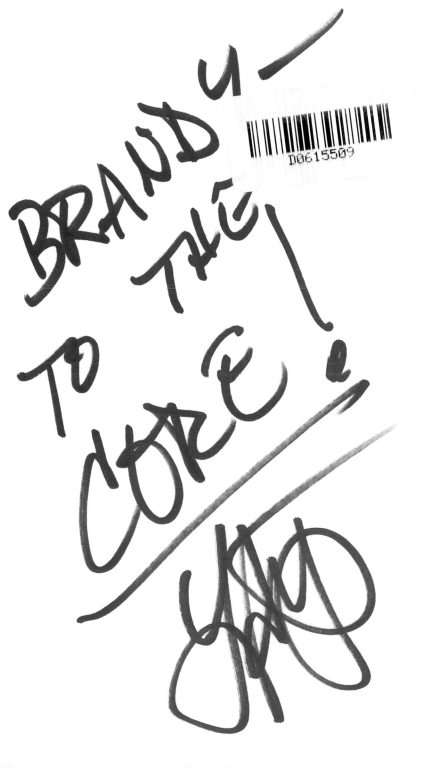

BRANDY —
TO THE
CORE

ID615509

What's Wrong With
Damn Near
Everything!

What's Wrong With
Damn Near Everything!

How the Collapse of
Core Values is Destroying Us
and How to Fix It

LARRY WINGET

WILEY

Cover Design: Michael J. Freeland
Cover Image: Courtesy of Randall Bohl

Copyright © 2017 by Larry Winget. All rights reserved.

Published by John Wiley & Sons, Inc., Hoboken, New Jersey.
Published simultaneously in Canada.

No part of this publication may be reproduced, stored in a retrieval system, or
transmitted in any form or by any means, electronic, mechanical,
photocopying, recording, scanning, or otherwise, except as permitted under
Section 107 or 108 of the 1976 United States Copyright Act, without either
the prior written permission of the Publisher, or authorization through
payment of the appropriate per-copy fee to the Copyright Clearance Center,
222 Rosewood Drive, Danvers, MA 01923, (978) 750-8400, fax (978) 646-
8600, or on the web at www.copyright.com. Requests to the Publisher for
permission should be addressed to the Permissions Department, John Wiley &
Sons, Inc., 111 River Street, Hoboken, NJ 07030, (201) 748-6011, fax (201)
748-6008, or online at www.wiley.com/go/permissions.

Limit of Liability/Disclaimer of Warranty: While the publisher and author
have used their best efforts in preparing this book, they make no
representations or warranties with respect to the accuracy or completeness of
the contents of this book and specifically disclaim any implied warranties of
merchantability or fitness for a particular purpose. No warranty may be
created or extended by sales representatives or written sales materials. The
advice and strategies contained herein may not be suitable for your situation.
You should consult with a professional where appropriate. Neither the
publisher nor the author shall be liable for damages arising herefrom.

For general information about our other products and services, please contact
our Customer Care Department within the United States at (800) 762-2974,
outside the United States at (317) 572-3993 or fax (317) 572-4002.

Wiley publishes in a variety of print and electronic formats and by print-on-
demand. Some material included with standard print versions of this book may
not be included in e-books or in print-on-demand. If this book refers to media
such as a CD or DVD that is not included in the version you purchased, you
may download this material at http://booksupport.wiley.com. For more
information about Wiley products, visit www.wiley.com.

ISBN 9781119417026 (cloth); ISBN 9781119417040 (ePDF);
ISBN 9781119417071 (ePub)

Printed in the United States of America

10 9 8 7 6 5 4 3 2

CONTENTS

This Is Another Larry Winget Book   ix

Preface   xi

Chapter One. The Collapse of Core Values   1

What Are Core Values?   1

Finding Your Core Values   4

Why Have People Stopped Being Bothered?   5

Want to Know Why This Stuff Bothers You? It's Simple   8

Get Ready for Life to Be Much Easier for You!   9

A Test for Knowing Whether Something Is a Core Value   9

You Can Always Spot Someone's Core Values   10

Chapter Two. What's Wrong with People   13

From Today's News   14

People Cater to the Lowest Common Denominator   17

Let's Keep Digging into This   22

People Have Lowered Their Standards   23

People Are Self-Absorbed   28

People Either Can't, Don't, or Won't Manage Their Money   29

Why Most People Believe They Don't Have Money   31

Become Committed to Your Commitments   37

People Are Either Too Gullible or Too Skeptical   40

People Use Bad Grammar and Can't Spell   46

People Let Their Emotions Rule Their Lives 49
People Follow Their Dreams Instead of Going to Work 52
Starting Your Own Business Is Not a Dream, It's a
    Nightmare 52
Why Do Most Businesses Fail? Lack of Preparation 53
People Are Entitled 57
Entitlement Is the Enemy of Self-Reliance 60
The Government Is Feeding Entitlement Mentality 62
People Are Full of Excuses and Blame 67
People Are Dishonest and Lack Integrity 69
We Have Become Way Too Tolerant of Dishonesty 72
People Are Mean 76
Business Has Become Mean 77
People Are Lazy 80
People Are Disrespectful and Uncivil 84
Respect and Racism, Sexism, Ageism, Wealthism, and
    Homophobia 87
Respect Is Not Just about Respecting People 90
People Are Offended By Damn Near Everything! 93
Luckily Some People Are Speaking Up Against This
    Stupidity 104
People Allow Technology to Rule Their Lives 106

Chapter Three. What's Wrong with Business 109

Why Do Businesses Exist? 109
The Biggest Challenge Facing Business 112
Employees Must Constantly Add Value 116
Fiduciary Responsibility 118

Chapter Four. What's Wrong with Education 121

Parental Involvement 125
Failure *Is* an Option 126
Beyond School Systems 129

Chapter Five. What's Wrong with Our
                     Government   131

Welcome to Helicopter America   131
Dear Government: Mind Your Own Business!   133
We Have Too Many Laws   134
Politics and Politicians   140

Chapter Six. The Big Question: Are We Able to
                     Turn All This Around?   147

In Your Business   148
In Your Family   148
In Your Own Life   149
Are You Willing to Live by These Core Values?   149
You Can't Change the World   150

About the Author   153

THIS IS ANOTHER LARRY WINGET BOOK

If you are a fan of my work or have read any of my six best-selling books, listened to or watched my speeches or online videos, or follow me on social media, then much of what I say in this book is not going to be new to you. When it comes to some of this stuff, I am a broken record. That's one of the reasons I am called The Pitbull of Personal Development®; I grab on and don't let go—just like a pitbull.

That's because what I talk about and write about comes from my core values, my experience, and my research. These things don't change much from week to week or even year to year. They don't even change too much over a lifetime—some, but not much—and that is why all of it shows up in all that I do and say and write. So, if you are a fan, you are going to see some familiar ideas. But you are going to see a lot of new stuff here, too. Grittier stuff. More "I can't believe he said that" stuff. At least I hope so. I didn't hold back on any of it.

On the other hand, if you are completely new to my work, you are going to find out pretty quickly that I have very strong opinions, I don't mince words, and I say exactly what I believe without apology. And you will disagree with me a lot. To that I say, "good." If you disagree, then you are engaged. There is nothing better than becoming engaged by new and different ideas. Embrace it. Enjoy it. Even when you hate what I've said and end up hating me because I've said it, that's okay because you will have more clarity about what you believe by reading what I believe.

By the way, if you are one of those hypersensitive, smiley-face types who gets offended by blunt, straight talk that steps on your fragile little toes, you are in for a really rough ride.

Okay . . . giddy-up!

PREFACE

The first time I announced the title of this book to a group of people, there were a few who said, "Why do you have to be so negative? Why can't you write a book called, "What's right with darn near everything"? I laughed. That wouldn't be my style at all. Most importantly, it's not what's right that is our problem; it's what's wrong that we aren't doing a damn thing about that is our problem. In this book, I'm not going to spend much time on what's right, instead I'm going to spend my time talking about what's wrong, why it's wrong, and what we can do about it.

Face it: things are a mess. I bet you will find it hard to argue with that statement. Our government is a mess: it's too big, it costs too much, and for the most part, it's ineffective. You can top that off with the fact that people have completely lost confidence in it and the politicians who run it. Recent polling says that 68 percent of people believe we are headed in the wrong direction.

It's not just government; businesses are a mess, too. Many have forgotten that businesses exist to fill a need, solve a problem, serve their customers well, and be profitable while doing it. A strong work ethic in employees has become a thing of the past. Too many leaders confuse leadership with popularity.

Families are no exception, either. Too many parents are indulgent, overprotective, and don't communicate or teach morals, ethics, or values. They are raising narcissistic brats who have no respect for others or for themselves. And while the economy is a mess in our country, it's simply a reflection of the disastrous way we handle our own money as individuals and in our families. People spend money they don't have buying things they don't need to impress people they don't like.

Individuals blame instead of taking responsibility. They rationalize their behavior. They are personally offended by almost everything even when it has nothing to do with them. They demand things, believing they are entitled to them instead of earning them. We even have a huge segment of society that has moved back in with their parents instead of sucking it up and figuring out how to make it on their own. They put more thought and more money into their grande half-caf Mochachino Frappuccino Crapacino than they do their savings accounts. They distract themselves with social media instead of working. I could go on and on and on, and every one of you reading this could add 50 more statements that would be true about what a mess people have become.

Education might be the area where it is the worst. College campuses are now full of safe zones where grown men and women can run and hide to protect themselves from the hurtful words of others. And yes, 18 years old is grown. We have 18-year-old men and women dying while defending our country so I consider 18-year-olds grown. Colleges have become bastions of uber-liberal ideas that charge exorbitant amounts of money to nurture oversensitivity instead of challenging thinking and encouraging growth.

Some of us wake up every day and read or watch the news and barely recognize the world we *live in*. And some of us never read anything and only watch *Keeping Up with the Kardashians* or *The Bachelor* or other drivel and are totally clueless about the world we live in.

Is all of what I've said here a series of broad, sweeping generalizations? Of course! But that doesn't make the statements any less true. They don't apply to everyone but they apply to more than enough. I recognize there are exceptions to each of these points. Not all leaders, families, businesses, schools, or government officials are a mess. But those are the exception and not the rule. I hope you are one of the exceptions to every one of the statements I've made. However, whether you are the exception to these statements or whether you are the epitome of one of these statements, you are going to have to admit that I'm right: things are a mess!

To be very, very clear: I am not saying that nothing is going right. I am not ignoring or discounting all of the good in the world. I see it. I acknowledge it. I applaud it. But that is not what this book is about. This book is not about what is going right. This book is about what is going wrong and what we must do to fix it. I am a firm believer that it is impossible to fix a problem unless you recognize and identify your issue as a problem, then go to work to fix it.

And we are already making some efforts to fix these things. But I believe that for the most part, we are going about fixing things backward. We are working at fixing things from the outside in. That rarely works and it is typically a temporary fix at best. You almost always create long-term change when you fix things from the inside out. But that requires more time and energy and sweat than most people are willing to invest.

We are building walls around our country to keep the bad guys out. And while I think that is a fine idea, we have bad guys we have created right here that are doing us just as much harm simply because parents are teachers and society didn't take the time to do the work to teach people that valuing life and respecting others and not committing crimes is a better way to live.

We are also building walls around our personal beliefs, ideals, biases, and prejudices. We create safe zones to protect us from the harmful words of others, instead of teaching people to be strong enough to withstand harmful words and kind enough not to say harmful words. To make matters worse, we have redefined a harmful word to mean anything you don't agree with. And while I agree that our individual rights should be protected, it seems that we only want protection for *our* rights, not the rights of anyone who disagrees with us.

We don't allow kids to play tag, hide-and-seek, or other games—or in some cases even have outside recess because they might get hurt. Or worse, their feelings might get hurt. We have even gone so far in some cities as to pay criminals not to commit crimes. Again, this is just an external solution to an internal problem. How about letting kids know that you don't always get picked and when you play, sometimes you get hurt. How about teaching people not to be criminals instead of rewarding them for being a criminal.

Our outer world is collapsing and needs to be fixed, no doubt about it. But as the old saying goes, "As within, so without." Our outer world is only a reflection of our inner world. Our outer world is a mess because we are a mess.

I do believe we are facing the collapse of society, but it won't be because of the government, the liberals, the conservatives, ISIS, foreign enemies, the economy, obesity, cigarettes, drugs, or any other external factor. Our society will collapse if we continue to let our core values collapse. We have to fix the issues I am going to discuss in this book. However, here is the problem:

People typically only take action to fix their problem when it's damn near too late.

My goal is that people read this book, realize how bad things are, and decide to take action to fix things before it's too late.

CHAPTER ONE

THE COLLAPSE OF CORE VALUES

WHAT ARE CORE VALUES?

When I want to figure out what something *is*, I often begin by figuring out what it *isn't*. That's how I determined the definition of what a core value is for this book.

In researching the definitions of core values, I discovered what others have expressed to be their core values. I looked at what various companies and organizations and individuals said their core values were. I saw lots of words like teamwork, passion, enthusiasm, punctuality, safety, fun, flexibility, ethics, love, creativity. These are all fine words, but none are core values.

These words might be principles for your life or business to practice. Some are simply ideals. Some are just nice things to say on your company website for your customers to read. But they are not core values by my definition.

Core values are different from traditional values. The idea of traditional values has been hijacked by various political and religious groups using those words to promote their particular beliefs. You won't find any of those things mentioned here. For me, core values run deeper.

So for more help on what a core value is, I went to some of the published definitions:

According to yourdictionary.com, the definition of core value is:

> The core values are the guiding principles that dictate behavior and action. Core values can help people to know what is right from wrong; they can help companies to determine if they are on the right path and fulfilling their business goals; and they create an unwavering and unchanging guide.

According to BusinessDictionary.com, the definition of core value is:

> A principle that guides an organization's internal conduct as well as its relationship with the external world.

On the website for the National Park Service, they answer the question, "What are core values?" with these words:

> Core values are not descriptions of the work we do or the strategies we employ to accomplish our mission. The values underlie our work, how we interact with each other, and which strategies we employ to fulfill our mission. The core values are the basic elements of how we go about our work. They are the practices we use (or should be using) every day in everything we do.

I also like The Four-Way Test of Rotary International from rotary.org:

> The Four-Way Test is a nonpartisan and nonsectarian ethical guide for Rotarians to use for their personal and professional relationships. The test has been translated into more than 100 languages, and Rotarians recite it at club meetings:
>
>   Of the things we think, say, or do
>
> - Is it the *truth*?
> - Is it *fair* to all concerned?
> - Will it build *goodwill* and *better friendships*?
> - Will it be *beneficial* to all concerned?"

These definitions are more closely aligned with my views. I especially like the idea that core values create unwavering and unchanging guides that determine everything we do.

I contend that most people haven't spent much time determining the unwavering, unchanging guides that direct everything they do. For the most part, neither have most businesses. Or most churches. Or most schools. Neither has society.

To be clear, I'm not talking about rules or regulations. And I'm not talking about laws. There is no shortage of rules, regulations, or laws and we are still in a mess. So, obviously, the fix to our problems is not more laws for society or rules and regulations for our businesses. It has to go deeper.

What are your core values? Have you ever given it much thought? Do you even know where to start?

FINDING YOUR CORE VALUES

Stuff bothers me. Sometimes, stuff bothers me a lot! As you read this book, that fact will become completely evident to you. But here is something I firmly believe:

It's not what bothers you that matters,
it's what has stopped bothering you.

I never want to reach the point that things stop bothering me. Too many have done that already. By the way, I completely understand that the made-up world is sometimes more attractive than the one we actually live in and that we all need an escape from time to time. I get it. But you can't fix the real problems of the real world when you stop paying attention or bury your head in the sand. And in this case, sand means five hours of television per day and nine hours of playing on your device (i.e. your phone, iPad, or laptop).

I care about things and want them to get better. Because of that, I consciously work at staying bothered, although it really doesn't take much work. I know that flies in the face of some of what many of you believe. If you like a world of nothing but positivity and your Facebook cover photo is a unicorn with a rainbow, then you are going to think, "How sad, Larry; you work at being bothered," all while shaking your pretty little head and saying, "tsk, tsk." Yes, I do work at staying bothered. Because when I stop being bothered by injustice, dishonesty, a lack of integrity, and by what is wrong in the world, I will stop bothering to try to make it better. I couldn't live with myself if I just stopped bothering to make things better.

Yet, that seems to be what has happened. People aren't much bothered and they aren't bothering to fix the few things that are bothering them. Parents have stopped bothering to teach their kids about life and money and respect and how to be self-sufficient. Managers have stopped bothering to make sure employees come in on time. They have stopped being bothered by missed commitments and upset customers. The government has stopped bothering with creating jobs and expecting people to take care of themselves because it's easier to just write them a check not to work rather than going to the trouble of creating jobs so they can go to work. Overall, people and institutions have stopped being bothered with the mess we are in except to complain about it.

What I hear from most folks is a whole lot of "oh well" when what I really would love to hear is "oh *hell* no!"

WHY HAVE PEOPLE STOPPED BEING BOTHERED?

Maybe it's because they feel things are so bad that they're too far gone to fix.

Maybe it's because they don't know where to start.

Maybe it's because they don't know what to do to fix what's wrong.

Maybe it's because they never gave much thought to what was causing the problem so they just can't comprehend how all this could happen.

Maybe they have resigned themselves to the idea that the world is going down the tubes anyway, so nothing they do is going to make any difference. After all, how much difference can one person really make in the big scheme of things?

Maybe it's because they got lured into the idea that things aren't as bad as the Pollyanna liberal media or the mean-spirited conservative media (take your pick) has made it out to be. (I actually believe it is much worse than any of the media sources have made it out to be.)

Maybe it's because they honestly don't care about what happens. There really are people who don't care. They live in their own little world and as long as it doesn't affect them personally, they don't care what's going on. I hear these excuses all the time: "I don't have any money in the stock market, so I don't care." "I don't vote so it doesn't matter to me who the president is." "I'm old and not going to be around much longer, so I don't care what happens to the planet."

Maybe it's because they are lazy. Way too many recognize the problem and know they could contribute to fixing it but are just too lazy to put out any effort to turn things around.

Maybe it's because they are afraid to speak up. Sadly, too many people just won't speak up for fear of being ridiculed, made fun of, or put down in some way. Speaking up and expressing their opinion might offend someone and they certainly don't want to do that.

And maybe, just maybe, it's that they think we are headed in the right direction.

This last group scares me the most. And there are plenty of people in this category. I hear from them every day. They tell me that my thoughts on personal responsibility and doing the right thing and being committed to paying my bills are old school. I regularly get hate mail in which people wish horrible things on me, my health, and even my family just because I take a stand for what they consider to be outdated, silly values. They argue that the country is finally starting to turn around and care about others and about the planet and about eating right. They claim that we are finally becoming a caring society of people with expanded consciousness instead of greedy, capitalistic slaves to corporate thinking.

Horseshit. Yep, let's get it said early and call it what it is. We aren't nearly as nice to others or about others as we pretend to be. People always overestimate their own "goodness." I say that you can be rich and they say that you should be abundant, and because they claim to be spiritual it is as if their money is somehow better than mine. It's called being self-righteous, and no one is better at it than we have become. Remember, we are the society that will push people down and kick them on Black Friday to save $10 on a pair of Air Jordans.

The ridiculous notion that the world is becoming a better place is nothing but an ill-informed distraction to rationalize our lack of values.

Our values are slipping and it shows up in every area of our society, and it terrifies me that people have convinced themselves this isn't the case.

Let's figure out what your values are. It's not that hard; all you have to do is figure out what is bothering you.

So what bothers you? Seriously, I want to know exactly what bothers you? Unless you articulate it, write it down, and make a commitment to doing your small part in fixing it, it's just complaining. So take a few moments and find a sheet of paper and write down what bothers you most.

WANT TO KNOW WHY THIS STUFF BOTHERS YOU? IT'S SIMPLE

Things that don't bother you at all are not in conflict with your core values. Things that bother you a lot are in big conflict with your core values.

Stop for a moment and think on that idea.

Things bother you in direct proportion to how much they are in conflict with your core values.

The things that piss me off the most are the things that go against my core values the most. I can't tolerate being lied to. You simply don't get to lie to me. Not twice for sure. That is because honesty is one of my core values. People are lied to all the time and it doesn't seem to bother them. Why is that? It's because honesty isn't a core value to them. And that's probably because they are liars themselves.

I can't stand it when people are late. I can't stand being late. I would never tolerate an employee being late as it goes against my core values of respect and integrity. Yet, people showing up late isn't an issue for many individuals. I never could understand that until I realized that those people are late too, so they don't see it as an issue when someone else is. It doesn't violate any of their core values.

Go back and look at your list of things that bother you. Now think of those things in terms of your core values. There is a good chance this is the first time you even realized what your core values are. That's reason for celebration right there!

GET READY FOR LIFE TO BE MUCH EASIER FOR YOU!

Once you know what your core values are, from that point on, everything will become much easier. It's easier for you to be a better parent, a better employee or employer, a better spouse or friend, and a better citizen. It will become easier for you to decide who to do business with and how to do business. It will be easier to parent your children. Easier to vote. Easier to handle your money. There is no area or life that is not touched and altered once you know your core values and start to live according to them.

When core values are clear, priorities are easy to set. When priorities are established, decision-making becomes easier.

A TEST FOR KNOWING WHETHER SOMETHING IS A CORE VALUE

If you are still struggling with whether something is a core value or just a strong belief you have about life or business, then understand this about a core value: You can't be talked out of a core value. No situation will change your mind. I couldn't hold a gun to your head and make you think differently. No amount of argument will make any difference. You will never compromise a core value.

YOU CAN ALWAYS SPOT SOMEONE'S CORE VALUES

I can look at your behavior and know what your core values are. I can drive down the road next to you and know what your core values are simply by the way you drive and treat others in traffic. I can watch the behavior of your kids and know exactly who you are and what you stand for. I can also do business with you and determine the core values of your company. I can tell this by the way your employees treat your customers, whether they greet them, offer to help them, and show appreciation for them. When people tell me they don't vote, they have helped me identify their core values. When people tell me they are broke, with no savings, I know their core values.

See how it works? It's become pretty simple for me because I have focused on this idea for many years. As you become more clear about your own core values, you will start to recognize the core values of others.

Your core values become the lenses
through which you see the world.

Now that you have some idea of what a core value is and how it impacts every area of your life and society, let me show you what the collapse of core values has done to us. The title of the book is "What's Wrong with Damn Near Everything," so let's get right to what I believe is wrong.

CHAPTER TWO

WHAT'S WRONG WITH PEOPLE

"What the hell is wrong with people?" I have pondered this question for years. I used to just think people were idiots. In fact, I wrote a *New York Times* bestseller called *People Are Idiots and I Can Prove It*. That was the easiest book I have written. The evidence is everywhere for just how idiotic the average person's behavior has become.

So what *is* wrong with people? Let me count the ways.

People make lousy decisions.

Our decisions create our reality. Rarely does stuff just happen to us. Things happen to us because we made a decision that put a chain reaction in place that resulted in what we ended up with.

If you choose to spend more money than you have, you end up broke.

If you choose to smoke cigarettes and not take care of yourself, you end up dead.

If you choose to treat your spouse like crap, you end up divorced.

If you choose to show up late to work and be a slacker, you end up unemployed.

If you choose to treat customers poorly, you end up with no customers and go out of business.

FROM TODAY'S NEWS

As I am typing this, I am watching the morning news. I see a story about a person standing in a lagoon in Florida with the result being he was eaten by an alligator. How could this possibly happen? No signage!!! Obviously, signage is the problem! By blaming the lack of signage, it makes being eaten by an alligator in a Florida swamp someone else's responsibility.

Next is a story about Arizona considering enacting a Stupid Hiker Law. You see, it gets to be 120 degrees here, and people decide to hike our beautiful mountain trails with little or no water. Then they collapse and sometimes die. The city or state spends tens of thousands of dollars on firefighters and rescue teams traveling up the mountain or sending a helicopter to bring these people out. So they are about to close the trails during the hottest hours. This, of course, would require money to hire people to build a gate and then show up to close a gate and open a gate to every trail (we have hundreds) to protect people stupid enough to believe that hiking in 120 degree heat without adequate hydration is a fine idea. Or maybe they will just put up signage that says it's too hot to hike today. Yeah, that'll work as we all know that signs and notices always stop people from doing stupid things. After all, that cancer warning put on cigarette packaging in 1966 sure stopped people from smoking didn't it?

The other story is about 40 people burning their feet after walking on hot coals at a Tony Robbins firewalk event in Dallas. Evidently these fine folks were surprised they got their feet burned after walking on hot coals at a *firewalk* event! What the hell did you expect to happen, Einstein? Even dumber than walking on hot coals is thinking that doing so will somehow motivate you to do better in life by overcoming your fears. Seems to me that you should be afraid to walk on hot coals because the evidence suggests that when you try to overcome fear and prove yourself brave by stepping onto red-hot coals, you get your stupid feet burned!

Sadly, this is a typical news day by most accounts. People wander into a swamp and get eaten by an alligator, go hiking with no water on a 120-degree day and walk across hot coals expecting that all will be fine. In my opinion, this is just culling the herd. If you are unfamiliar with the term, TheFreeDictionary says to "cull the herd" is to separate or remove (and usually kill) inferior animals from a herd so as to reduce numbers or remove undesirable traits from the group as a whole.

That's the way nature works. The inferior are removed. They are too slow to keep up, so the predator attacks and removes them. Works that way in the wild very well. Works that way with humans, too. The stupid are removed not so much by predators but by their own stupidity.

Now am I saying these people deserved to die? No, of course not. I am not a cruel person who enjoys it when people die even when they do stupid things. However, actions have consequences. Understanding the consequences of stupid actions in advance of doing those stupid actions can certainly save you from lots of pain and suffering. (By the way, I am saying that those people did deserve to get their feet burned.)

The problem is that in our overprotective society the weak want the government to protect them from everything and anything by posting signs and passing more laws to remove all personal responsibility. To facilitate blame and to provide a vehicle to abdicate personal responsibility is enabling. To enable others is cruelty; to expect responsible behavior is kindness.

If you eat too much you will get fat and your chances of dying from it are likely. Obesity-related diseases are the number-one killer in the United States.

If you smoke, the likelihood of dying from a smoking-related disease goes way up. Smoking-related diseases are the number-two killer in the United States.

We don't need legislation to protect you from smoking and eating. We didn't legislate that you should smoke and overeat, and it's ridiculous to legislate that you shouldn't. What you do with your body is your business. The government should have no say in it. While I bet many of you agree with my position, do you agree with it to the point where you are willing to take full responsibility for your actions? Or do you want to do stupid things and have the taxpayer pay for your stupid decisions?

Why should I pay for the consequences of your decisions with my tax dollars? I don't believe I should. I know that in some of your minds this appears to be a callous and uncaring statement. It just might be. However, if you do something that you know will likely kill you and you get sick from it or even die from it, I don't feel particularly responsible for you in any way. Your decisions and your actions equal your consequences. I'm out. Yes, I feel bad for anyone who suffers. I don't like to see people suffer for any reason. And I certainly hate it when others suffer as a result of someone else's bad decisions. I care when I see kids whose parents die from a heart attack or from diabetes because they didn't push back from the table when they should have . . . for 40 years. Of course I care. I just wonder why *they* didn't care enough to make sure that it didn't happen.

Decisions have consequences. Actions have consequences. If you make a good decision and take intelligent action, chances are pretty good that the consequences will be good. If you make a bad decision and take stupid action, chances are pretty good that the consequences will be bad. The earlier we teach people this and let them learn that their decisions and actions have consequences, the faster they will learn the importance of making better decisions and taking smarter action. When we cheat kids and everyone else from feeling the pain of their consequences and allow them to blame others for their mistakes, they will never learn. By the way, we are there already and now we have some backtracking to do in order to turn things around.

PEOPLE CATER TO THE LOWEST COMMON DENOMINATOR

From the beginning of business, many leaders and managers have spent most of their time, energy, and money catering to the worst employees trying to save them. In doing so, they practically abandon the top performers and the people who want help and could actually benefit from some leadership. Some people simply want to be at the bottom, otherwise they would show up and do the work. They don't want to be the best, they just want to be paid like the best and enjoy the same perks as the best. These folks are perfectly satisfied and comfortable being lousy performers and couldn't care less about you wasting your time trying to develop them. Don't argue this point; it's true and I'm right. Solution? Fire them.

Businesses must stop this dumb practice of catering to the lousy employees while sacrificing good employees in the name of being fair. There is nothing fair about performance. If you perform well on your job, serving both the customer and the company through your hard work and great attitude, then you should be rewarded more than a whiney slacker. And it doesn't matter what color they are, how old they are, what gender they are, or how long they have worked there. Businesses must get back to rewarding performance. Great performers get the perks. Lousy performers get the boot. And government should keep its stupid nose out of businesses doing this. It is none of the government's business who gets fired. In fact, the government should pay attention to what I am saying here and fire every incompetent employee it employs, even though I'm sure it would leave us with less than half of the employees on the payroll now. Wait—wouldn't that be a good thing?

Catering to the worst employees sends the wrong message to the top employees and to customers of the company. I want to know that the companies I spend my money with care more about me than they do their bad employees.

I recently made a reservation with a major high-end hotel chain. I had a special request of an early check-in and a late checkout (which I was more than willing to pay for), so I wasn't able to make the reservation online and had to phone the reservation number in order to talk to a real live person. And that's what I got: a real live brain-dead person. The reservations agent took all of the information from me, assured me that he understood what I wanted, had done as I requested, and while I was on the phone with him, sent me an e-mail confirmation. As I looked at the e-mail reservation I realized that every bit of it was wrong. Wrong size room. The price was different than he quoted. Nothing in the reservation about early check-in or late checkout. When I questioned him about the difference in what I asked for and what he had assured me that he had done for me versus what the reservation confirmed, he told me that he had no power or ability to change it or fix it after the confirmation e-mail was sent. I said, "But you got it wrong!" And without another word, he transferred me to the customer service department. Now, I have a new person that I have to start over with to fix an incorrect reservation made by a totally incompetent employee. In explaining my frustration to this new very nice woman, I asked her why I was even talking to her since the other guy knew what I wanted and had done it wrong. I wanted to know why he didn't just fix it. She said, "My department fixes their mistakes." I was astounded. I said, "So your department exists to fix the mistakes of the department I just talked to that got it wrong?" She told me that was correct. I asked if her department employed a lot of people and she assured me it did. I asked her if her department was busy and she said every person at every desk was answering calls 24/7, 365 days a year. I asked her, "Why doesn't your company just teach the people in the first department to do things right and when they don't, allow them to fix their own mistakes? Seems like that would save them a lot of money and save the customer a lot of frustration." She said that made too much sense for her company to do. Sheesh.

The lousy performer wins, the company spends more than it has to on employees, and the customer ends up the loser.

But it's not just in business. We cater to the lowest common denominator in sports, too.

In Minnesota, a girls basketball team was kicked out of its league for being too good. Yep, you read it right. The Rogers Area Youth Basketball Association girl's high school team was forced out of its league because its skill level was so far above that of the other teams in the Northwest Suburban Basketball League. Talent, practice, dedication, and hard work be damned! It appears they wanted the teams with lower skills to have more of a chance at winning, and the team that worked the hardest to be good needed to play worse to make that happen. How is that fair to those girls who worked hard to win their games? How is that fair to the teams that don't play as well? Where is their incentive to get better? What goes on in the minds of people who make these kinds of decisions? What lesson is this teaching these young girls about winning, losing, and fairness?

Remember when Tiger Woods was winning nearly every golf tournament he played in? Can you imagine telling Tiger to play worse so the other players would have more of a chance?

How about Muhammad Ali? "Hey Ali, let the other guy have a few rounds just to give him and other fighters hope they can eventually beat you."

How about your favorite team? Do you want those players to play worse so other teams can have a better chance at beating them?

Here's one for you: How about we tell Apple it's selling too many iPhones and needs to slow down in order to let Samsung catch up. How fair would that be to the stockholders? To the customers? To anyone involved?

Doesn't all of this strike you as unbelievably stupid? What happened to competition? What about working to get better? Aren't we undermining the goal of having everyone work to be his very best? Or is that even our goal these days? It seems that our goal is to never hurt anyone's feelings for not being as good at something as another person. It seems that we are more interested in making everyone feel good than inspiring them to perform well. That's why every kid gets a trophy. It's why kids get a passing grade when they should be failed.

In the real world, you fail. I have many times. I have failed at nearly every task I ever set out to do, whether it be in relationships, as a parent, as an employee, an employer, or a business owner. Those failures are what taught me and inspired me to do better. I am betting the same applies to you. But when we constantly cater to the lowest level and let people get by with mediocrity and lousy performance, we kill that drive to do better in our society, and our society, businesses, schools, and citizens will all pay the price down the road. Failure is the greatest teacher of success. Rob people of failure and we rob them of the lesson.

Most of the time, you have to get negative about your life in order to create positive change in your life. Parents and schools should be totally honest and teach their children the lessons that come with bad grades and then help them learn their lessons.

LET'S KEEP DIGGING INTO THIS

How about the Occupy Movement? Remember that? These folks protest against what they consider to be economic inequality. Their goal is socialism, where all people, regardless of contribution, receive the same. They don't want there to be wealthy people and poor people and people in the middle class. Their goal is a completely flat economy where all have the same, regardless of contribution. Their goal is a completely level playing field.

I don't want a level playing field. I want a *fair* playing field. I want a society where the opportunity exists for all to win. Where if you work hard enough and long enough and provide enough value to the marketplace you can do well. And I don't want the government picking winners and losers. I want results to determine who wins and who loses. And I want the marketplace to decide.

Ironic how the groups that demand more benefits and laws and support unions that rape companies don't have a clue that they are part of the cause of the very problem they protest against.

By the way, "Hey Mom and Dad, take a few minutes with your kids to teach them about capitalism and socialism. Help us all out a bit would you?"

We cater in the same way to every small group of people who scream and yell demanding that the whole world cater to them and their whims.

Fat? Outlaw fattening foods. Outlaw big soft drinks.

Lung cancer? Outlaw tobacco.

Can't get a job after college? Sue the university.

Aren't skilled enough to win? Blame the winner.

Poor? Blame the rich.

Broke? It's the credit card company's fault.

Can't spell or read or add and subtract? Blame the school.

Your feelings are hurt? It's my fault.

Buy a house you can't afford? Walk away and blame the bank.

Lead an unhealthy lifestyle and get sick? No problem, the rest of us will pay for your choices.

When we stop catering to the ignats and start expecting more, no, *demanding* more from everyone they just might, maybe, possibly (though probably won't) start to take personal responsibility.

PEOPLE HAVE LOWERED THEIR STANDARDS

In my book *It's Called Work for a Reason* I wrote about the old saying, "Good enough, ain't." Sadly, that no longer applies to almost every area of society, business, and people's lives. "Good enough is plenty" seems to be the new slogan. In fact, "Barely good enough to get by is more than enough" is more like it in most cases.

We let businesses get by with lousy service. We tolerate poor performance from people and companies we pay our money to. We tolerate bad behavior from our employees, other people, and even our own children. Why? Guess we just don't give a damn or at least enough of a damn to change things. It just takes too much effort. We live by the credo: "Not my circus and not my monkey."

Why get involved?

Why bother?

Who cares?

Let it slide.

It's no big deal.

Chill out.

Don't worry about it.

It doesn't matter that much.

What difference does it make?

Move on.

Get over it.

Uhhh . . . *No*. It matters!

What you tolerate, you endorse.
What you put up with, you condone.

I don't put up with bad behavior. I call people out on their shit. Why? Because to tolerate it is to endorse it and to put up with it is to condone it. Do you condone lying? No? Then why do you put up with it? Do you endorse rudeness? No? Then why do you tolerate it? Do you condone stealing? No? Then why do put up with employees who steal time from you? Should I keep going? Is my point made? I thought so.

If you put up with the degradation of society without speaking up about it and against it, then you are admitting to all that you condone and endorse it. I refuse.

In my industry, the personal development business, I watch speakers and authors steal material from others, claim it as their own, and then proclaim themselves to be thought leaders. Hell, they aren't even good thought followers. They are thieves. I call them out for that stuff whenever I see it. It's my profession I am standing up for, and I respect it enough to demand better from people who claim to be professionals in my industry. Besides, to be a thought leader, you need to have had an original thought.

I watch these bozos claim bestseller status for their self-published book when all it did was hit a subcategory of a subcategory of a subcategory of a category of books on Amazon. The people who do this are hacks and liars. By the way, folks, Amazon isn't a recognized bestseller list and all it takes to achieve number one in a subcategory is to sell about 10 books in the course of a one-hour period. Recently, a guy took a picture of his foot and uploaded it to Amazon and turned it into an Amazon number-one bestseller in a matter of minutes. Sound ridiculous? It is ridiculous. And it's 100 percent true. Be careful of the ridiculous claims people make, and when you catch them lying, call them out on it!

I saw another guy claim to be the number-one motivational speaker in the United States. I contacted him and asked him who compiled the list and for a copy of it as I couldn't find it anyplace. I asked him where Zig Ziglar, Tony Robbins, Brian Tracy, and a host of other friends of mine in the speaking business appeared on the list. I even asked him if I made the list since I have been doing this pretty successfully for 25 years. This guy has only been in the business for three years and claims to have reached millions of people and given thousands of speeches and built a multimillion-dollar business. I asked him how it was physically possible to have given thousands of speeches in three years. He wrote me a snarky reply saying, "I'm just doing what I said I would do, when I said I would do it, the way I said I would do it." The asshat used my own quote to justify his dishonest actions. I guess what he said he was going to do, when he said he was going to do it, and the way he said he was going to do it was to make up a fake list and lie about his credentials. He then banned me from being able to contact him and kept on posting his lies. He still is.

Is this going on just in my business? No. You have the same thing going on in your industry. Do you let the charlatans in your industry get by with it? Why? Have your standards dropped to the point that you just can't be bothered by the lies and deceit of others? Don't you want to protect the integrity of your industry? If you are tolerating it, you are condoning it. Call them out.

Why do we allow this? Wait, let me help you:

Why bother?
Who cares?
Let it slide.
It's no big deal.
Chill out.
Don't worry about it.
It doesn't matter that much.
What difference does it make?
Move on.
Get over it.

There's that damn list again!

If honesty and integrity are your core values, you are obligated to stand up for them.

I suggest you raise your standards and get a backbone right now. Stop tolerating lies and deceit and all of the half-truths people use about themselves, their achievements, and their businesses. A half-truth is still a whole lie. Yes, it takes effort. Yes, it can be a pain in the ass. Yes, people will condemn you for it. But know that when you stand up for something, stop accepting bad behavior, speak up, and have higher standards then you have done your part in making the world a better place for all of us.

A half-truth is still a whole lie.

A great example of how hard it is to live a life of high standards is in the miniseries *Lonesome Dove*, based on Larry McMurtry's book by the same name. In my opinion, it is the greatest thing ever put on film. If you haven't seen it, do. In the story, Woodrow Call, Gus McCrae, and Jake Spoon are famous Texas Rangers. Jake went off on his own for a while and, in the process, rode along with some very bad guys who included him in the stealing of some horses. He didn't steal the horses but he was there and didn't do anything to stop it, either. Woodrow and Gus catch them all and are faced with inflicting justice on the lot of them. The dilemma is that their best friend, Jake, is part of the group. As Jake pleads for his life, Gus says to him, "You know how it works, Jake. You ride with an outlaw, you die with an outlaw. I'm sorry, you crossed the line." They hang him along with the other thieves. They feel terrible about it, but they are men of such high standards they are willing to hang their friend. Great lesson there: doing the wrong thing carries consequences even though it is painful to inflict them.

PEOPLE ARE SELF-ABSORBED

I will be speaking much about the entitlement culture in this book, but let me briefly touch on the root cause here. People actually believe that it's all about them. They believe the place they go to work is there to serve them instead of the other way around. They believe the entire earth revolves around them.

The earth does indeed revolve . . . but not around you.

We would all be amazed to find out just how little people think about us at all. And it's almost never about you. You just think it is always about you because you don't have the ability to think about anyone or anything except yourself.

No one gives a damn about you. Don't cry. It's true. Oh, your momma and daddy do and possibly some of your family and a handful of friends. But know that could all change in a nanosecond if you continue to be an asshat and become too much of a pain to put up with. The faster you realize that people don't care about you and really only care about the value you bring to them, the better off you will be.

You aren't special. I wrote in my book, *Your Kids Are Your Own Fault*, that one of the biggest mistakes parents make is telling their children they are special. Some folks read that and their heads nearly exploded. "Of course my kids are special." Yes they are. To you. Only to you. They certainly aren't to me. And they aren't special to anyone else, either.

Your kids are special to you by birthright. But the instant they walk out the front door, it ceases to be about them as individuals and becomes only about their contribution.

However, the damage has already been done. These children have been told they were special and treated as if they were special and taught that everyone should treat them like they are special from the time they were born. Then the school system, under the influence of these delusional parents, feeds the self-absorption, and by the time the kid graduates from high school, there is no recovery. Then the marketplace and you and I are stuck with these pitiful people who expect to be coddled and hugged and told they are special at every turn. We are expected to understand and embrace them when they hold marches for their rights. Funny, the rights most of them march about aren't rights at all. I guess they march for the right to be treated special.

"Not true, Larry!! I am special to lots of people! And thousands of people care about me! Look at how many friends and followers I have on Facebook, Twitter, and Instagram! Look at how many people like everything I post!!!" Yep, people think like that. They measure their value and self-worth by their social media following. They believe that big numbers and lots of likes mean they are special. How truly pitiful.

PEOPLE EITHER CAN'T, DON'T, OR WON'T MANAGE THEIR MONEY

People are profoundly ignorant (don't know any better) and stupid (know better but don't care) when it comes to their money. They spend more than they have. For the most part they don't save. They don't invest. They spend their money on stupid things with little value. They live in the moment. They have no plan for retirement. Want me to prove it? I would love to!

Some facts:

- Forty-three percent of Americans spend more money than they earn. So how do they get by? They are forced to dip into any savings they might have or rely on credit cards or lean on family or friends to help make ends meet.
- Thirty-eight million households in the United States live paycheck to paycheck, meaning they spend every dime of their paycheck every time they get it.
- Twenty-six percent of Americans have no savings set aside for an emergency. Almost half of Americans wouldn't be able to cover an unexpected expense of $100 or less. Do these people believe they are bulletproof and that nothing is ever going to happen to them? Haven't they heard that old truism, "Shit happens"? If you have any life experience at all, you know just how true that statement is. So how are you going to pay when something unexpected does happen? Put it on a credit card? Write a hot check and hope for the best? Pray? Let's see how that stuff works out for you.
- And how about retirement? Forget that for way too many folks. They better hope and pray that Social Security somehow has enough money left to

pay them when they are old enough to collect it. Thirty-six percent of adults don't have any retirement fund or even a plan for retirement. Believe it or not, more than a quarter of adults between the ages of 50 and 64 aren't saving anything for their "golden years." How golden are those years really going to be when you're broke?

It is irresponsible to be broke because you spent more than you had and didn't save anything. It's stupid, too. And for me, it violates my core values. Yet, it doesn't seem to bother a lot of people. Why is that? They were never taught the importance of earning, saving, investing, and being charitable. Their parents didn't take the time to teach them those four core aspects of money. And then when they got older, they never bothered to learn them on their own. Instead of learning about money, they learned to make excuses for not having any.

WHY MOST PEOPLE BELIEVE THEY DON'T HAVE MONEY

They believe they aren't paid enough. Lots of folks these days are demanding a wage increase so they can have a "living wage." I am just so tired of that term. Here's an idea: learn to live on the wage you are paid. "But Larry! You don't understand! A family of four can't live on minimum wage!" Yep, you are correct. That was never the intention of minimum wage to begin with. Minimum wage is for minimum skill-level jobs. If you want to make more than minimum wage, increase your skill level. Don't protest, don't complain about your employer, don't strike—just go out and become worth more. Show some initiative. Try harder. Show up early, stay late, do more than you are asked to do. Take a class to improve your skills. Ask your boss for more responsibility. Ask her for more training. In other words, be worth more.

If you want to be paid more, be worth more.

Some whiney-ass people will have a thousand reasons about how unfair that statement is. Too bad. I'm right and the whiners are wrong. People are paid exactly what they are worth according to the marketplace. Is it unfair? Sure it is. Cops and fire personnel and teachers are worth more than they get paid. But the marketplace has decided the value they bring, and the marketplace set their wages. So if you don't like those wages, don't take those jobs. I don't know of a cop (and I know many) who took the job thinking he was going to get rich. Or a teacher. So while the equation isn't always fair, it's still the way the system works. Blaming the system won't change the equation.

Rich bosses are the reason employees aren't paid enough. I am sick of hearing broke people feebly making this stupid argument. Yes, the person saying "Do you want fries with that?" makes about $8 an hour and the CEO of McDonald's makes millions. I know that. I see the huge wage discrepancy. So if you think that discrepancy is unfair, consider this: That CEO is responsible for 1.7 million employees, 35,000 restaurants in 118 countries, with 68 million customers per day. The employee mumbles, "Can I have your order?" then hands you a hamburger. I'm thinking there might be a reason for the wage difference. That isn't wealth inequality, that's value inequality. It's contribution to the marketplace inequality.

Employees who complain about how owners and stockholders make so much while they make so little need to understand that they have nothing at stake by comparison. They carry none of the risk that stockholders and owners and officers do. My message to those who want to make this weak argument is to use your head. Be more logical and get the emotions of families of four trying to make it on minimum wage out of your mind. Do a little research. Be informed before you cry about things. Oh yeah, and try a little healthy dose of "Grow the hell up!" I know that families who try to survive on minimum wage are struggling. I am fully aware. But the solution is not to pay them more money. The solution is for them to get more training and for there to be more jobs in the marketplace to hire them at that higher skill level. And you will never see more and higher paying jobs appear if you drain companies by raising wages for the people who have very few skills.

And on the subject of minimum wage: When you raise the wages of the person at the bottom, every single person up the chain must receive an increase. Chances are that the guy supervising the $8-an-hour employee makes $10. If you take minimum wage to $15 an hour, then the supervisor has to get an increase to $20. And his boss has to get an increase, too. You are the one who wanted it to be fair, so let's make it fair for everyone. And have these folks thought about who is going to pay for these higher wages? Take it out of profits? Profit margins are pretty thin for most industries as it is. So the customer is going to pay for all of this. That 99-cent menu that jumped a couple of years ago to $1.19 will need to become the $2.99 menu. And who orders off that menu? The people who make minimum wage. See the problem? Now their raise is gone. Raise wages and prices go up. Prices go up and the increases in wages are eaten up by the higher prices. To all of you bleeding hearts out there, try something logical for a change: do the math.

Don't spend your money paying off someone else's debt. Thirty-eight percent of loan cosigners end up paying part or all of the loan. Never cosign a loan for anyone. Especially your kids. Even student loans! Let them earn their own way, pay their own way, and save up for what they want or need. Don't end up destroying your own financial situation because you end up paying off the debt of a family member or friend. You will lose the money and chances are good that the relationship will be destroyed as well.

Things cost too much. Let's get really clear about this one: Things don't cost too much. Things cost what they cost. I don't like some prices, either. I can't do a damn thing about it except choose to pay the price or choose not to pay it. Since I can't change the amount of money things cost, I have decided not to complain about it. Tell me how much sense it makes to complain about something you have absolutely no control over. Besides, maybe the truth is that things don't cost too much, it's just that you can't afford them! Ouch! You can't afford it. Deal with it. The answer for you might be to figure out a way to do without things that don't matter so you can afford things that do matter. Or to save up and buy that thing you want. Perhaps the solution for you is to earn more. But whatever path you decide to pursue, don't bother complaining. No one wants to hear it as we all are paying the same amount.

Don't spend money on stupid things. There is a huge group of people who say they don't have enough money, and it's simply because they spend their money on stupid things. Let's look at just a few of the things Americans spend their money on that are stupid.

Smokers on average spend 7 percent of their total income on cigarettes. In New York, some lower income smokers spend up to 25 percent of their income on their smokes. Of course, let's say you can afford to smoke cigarettes and cost is not an issue for you. Is dying an issue for you? Every cigarette you smoke ends your life 11 minutes earlier than if you had never smoked. Worth it?

The average U.S. worker spends over $1,100 per year on coffee. That's too much. I even had a couple on my old A&E television show who spent over $600 a month at Starbucks yet couldn't pay their mortgage. That's dumb. No, that's beyond dumb, it's idiotic and shameful. And it is proof of how messed up our priorities are. Don't get me wrong, I love coffee. I drink a lot of it. But I either make my own or buy real coffee, not some goofy, flavored, expensive coffee-flavored drink that costs $5 or more. And while I can afford those expensive coffee drinks, I don't see it as a good use of my dollars. I am principled enough about my spending that I see what a ridiculous waste of money it is. If I buy a cup of coffee when on the road, I buy a cup of *coffee*. Most people don't know or don't remember what coffee really is: it's black stuff in a cup. Put in your own sugar or cream if you must and pay a dollar for it.

My issue with coffee is not just cost or flavors. It's our current obsession with it. It's our newest fad. People post pictures of it with the little trees and flowers and hearts in the foam. Their lives seem to revolve around it and I know their social media does. Some even claim it to be their drug of choice.

Coffee has taken over bookstores and other retail stores. I am pretty sure that soon we will see a Starbucks inside a Starbucks. People go to coffee shops to sit and talk and take up space while they claim to be working (yeah, right) on the Internet. I might be considered a mean, out-of-touch, old fuddy-duddy, but I really do believe that coffee needs to be relegated to its proper place in our lives so we can get back to some things that really matter, and I don't mean social media!

We spend more money eating out than on groceries. The average American spends about $1,000 per year just eating out at lunch. Not surprising to me is that millennials spend more eating out than nonmillennials. Sadly, amazingly, and stupidly, 87 percent of them are willing to splurge on an expensive meal even when money is tight. Folks, here is an idea: brown bag it for lunch. Eating at home is cheaper than eating out. Never splurge on anything expensive when money is tight. Don't even splurge on anything cheap when money is tight. Don't splurge at all when money is tight! Why does this even need to be explained?

Priorities: Needs. Wants. Can't-live-withouts. When money is an issue, and it is for most people, you have to think of every expenditure in those three categories. Start with the things you can't live without and then move to needs and then, after everything else, including after you have put at least 10 percent of your money in savings, you can move to wants. By the way, for you confused people, premium cable and the NFL package is not a need.

Care about your future. Two things you will never be without are your reputation and your credit rating. You can destroy both in an instant and spend the rest of your life trying to get them back. So many don't understand that fact at all. I got some feedback recently when I spoke about protecting your credit rating and a millennial told me she couldn't care less about her credit rating. That is a more widely embraced sentiment than I would have ever guessed. I told her that I hoped she never intended on buying anything on credit, getting insurance, or even getting a job. She told me she didn't. I shook my head in disbelief at her naiveté. Your credit rating proves that you have discipline in dealing with others. It is what communicates your commitment to your commitments. It speaks volumes about who you are.

BECOME COMMITTED TO YOUR COMMITMENTS

Every bill you have is a commitment. It's an obligation. Seems like way too many people no longer have a commitment to their commitments or understand what an obligation really is.

What are your commitments? Your family, your bills, and your word are your commitments.

When you take out a loan for your car or a mortgage for your house, you sign a contract promising you will pay them back. By the way, a credit card is a revolving loan and works the same way. You signed a contract saying you would pay a certain amount on a certain date to your credit card company. That contract is a legal document you must live up to.

Even more than it being a legally binding contract, it's a commitment. It's a deal. And a deal is a deal. Ever heard that before?

What that means is that you keep your commitments. Not convenient? Too bad, a deal is a deal. You spent the money on partying and you don't have the money to make your payment? You should have thought of that before you spent the money. I guess you won't be eating this week. Yes, I guess you won't be eating this week! Your personal needs don't come before your commitments. That's what it means to make a commitment. Nothing gets in the way. Nothing. You made a deal and you need to live up to the deal you made.

Pay your bills. No excuses. Pay them because you already enjoyed the benefits. You drove the car, you lived in the house, you wore the clothes, and you ate the food you bought on your credit card. You enjoyed the lights and the water. Don't be a deadbeat. Don't be a liar. And don't claim that honesty and integrity are important to you if you aren't going to exercise those core values in how you pay your bills.

By the way, being committed to your commitments isn't just about money. You committed to take care of your family. Do it. Do your best by them—it's what responsible, mature adults do. There are no excuses for not doing right by your kids. Doing right by your kids, however, does not mean that you support them into adulthood. Doing right by your kids means that you take the time to teach them the life skills necessary to do well in life. Your commitment to them is to do your best to raise productive adults who are good people, handle their money responsibly, are kind and generous, treat people fairly, and have a strong work ethic.

Now, become committed to doing your job to the best of your abilities. That is part of being committed to keeping your word. When you took the job, you told them you would be on time, work all the time you were on the job, and do your best every day. You said you would, so do it. If you don't, you are a liar. And you should be fired. By the way, companies are not nearly as guilty of not keeping their word as employees are. I know that is going to make some of you crazy and you will write me letters about it. Save yourself the time and trouble. If companies were as bad as some pain-in-the-ass employees complained about them being, all employees would be complaining. That is typically not the case. Typically, it is one or two employees who bitch and moan about how unfair their boss is or how unfair the working conditions are, not the majority of employees. In most cases, if those pain-in-the-ass employees had kept their word and done what they promised when being hired, the company wouldn't have a reason to enforce consequences.

As I talk about commitment, I want to add one more that you must become committed to: become committed to your own core values. Never compromise. They will be challenged. But just because you are challenged when you stand up for something doesn't mean you should sit down. Stand tall and firm in your commitment to your core values.

Just because you are challenged when you stand up for something doesn't mean you should sit down.

PEOPLE ARE EITHER TOO GULLIBLE OR TOO SKEPTICAL

Most people are either too gullible and believe everything or too skeptical and believe nothing.

When you consider the Tony Robbins scenario I mentioned earlier regarding his followers walking on fire and then move on to James Ray, whose followers went into a sweat lodge that ended up killing three people, you have to question just how much sense people have. Are you so weak that you can be talked into doing things that are physically harmful to yourself, putting life and limb at risk? If you are willing to walk on fire or go in a sweat lodge to overcome your fears, and you believe that having some charismatic bozo yelling at you will somehow benefit you in the long run, you need to stop and use your head. If you come to a Larry Winget seminar, you might get your feelings hurt but you won't get your feet burned and you won't die. My style is brusque and abrasive to some but my goal is to hold up a mirror to the behaviors of people so they will see how stupid they are being, then give them some ideas on how to be different. Not that bad, huh?

And it's not just body and life people risk to follow these charlatans; it can be money. There are people who will take your last dime. Some of them will do it with nothing more than a promise that you will find magnificent riches if you will just buy their program or attend their seminar. Of course, too many of these charlatans have only found their own riches by telling other people how to find their riches.

Be careful. Make sure that anything you invest your time and money in makes sense for you, your family, and your budget.

Don't be so quick to ask for help. Try fixing it yourself before you turn to someone else. Rely more on your own abilities. Sometimes asking for help is just an excuse not to learn how to do it. You don't need a life coach or a financial coach to tell you to spend less money than you earn. You don't need a health coach to tell you to exercise more or to eat less or to stop eating ice cream for breakfast. You should know this stuff even if you are a numbskull. Trust what you already know before you pay someone else your hard-earned money to remind you.

Here is the biggy when spending money with others for their help: Make sure these people have done what they are trying to talk you into doing. I see folks selling people into seminars about how to write a bestseller when they have never written one. Some will teach you how to get rich in real estate when they are so broke that they couldn't buy a ticket to their own seminar. Some promise to teach you how to get paid five figures to give a speech when they have never been paid that much themselves. Do your due diligence before pulling out your wallet.

Some rules for hiring or following mentors and coaches:

- Never spend money with anyone who has not done what they are attempting to teach you to do. Ask for proof.
- Talk to others to get testimonials to see if what they are teaching really works. Be fair, as everyone has participants who will claim the program didn't

work when in reality it was they who didn't do the work.

- Never expect to agree with 100 percent of what they say. You shouldn't agree 100 percent with anyone. However, just because you disagree with them doesn't make them wrong; it might just make that piece of advice wrong for you at this point in your life.

- Don't do anything that has the potential for causing you physical harm. You don't need to put your life at risk to find yourself, or overcome your fears, or discover your purpose (unless your purpose is to burn your feet).

- Don't spend your money on any program unless you are willing to do the work. A lot of the programs being sold really do work. However, they only work when you do the work. Don't buy the program, sit on your ass, then say that it was a bad program. You are to blame, not the program or the coach, just you.

Advice is plentiful; wisdom is in short supply.

Internet gullibility and stupidity: Not a day goes by that I don't open up my social media to see something that is so ridiculous that I know immediately that it can't be true. While that bugs me, it absolutely infuriates me when people share it like it's the gospel truth. Before you know it, it is all over the Internet and is assumed to be a true statement. Before you believe that someone is dead, or that your favorite actor committed some heinous crime, or that a politician said something outrageous about a group of people, or some ridiculous lawsuit got filed, or someone shared some fact about guns that isn't even remotely true, do some friggin' research! It might be true, but it could just as easily not be true. Take 10 seconds and do a fact check before you post it or share it. You are only adding to the stupidity of the human race by sharing lies and helping people jump to stupid conclusions when there are no facts involved.

Speaking of jumping to conclusions, when you see a crime video on television and you want to get all outraged and protest and raise hell about the injustice you have just seen, *wait*. A video is shot from one angle. There might be more to the story than you see with the limited view and short time frame of the video. You have no idea what happened before the camera started recording. Wait until the investigation is done. You might just end up being wrong. It has happened so many times recently where people jump to conclusions based on misinformation. People's lives can be ruined forever. Sometimes, people get hurt. Sometimes, people die. All because people overreact on unverified, uninvestigated, bad information. Wait until the investigation is done before you decide to protest or take the law into your own hands and end up committing a crime you can't come back from. Wait before you shoot your big mouth off on social media.

Regarding memes: I have close to a thousand memes on social media displaying my quotes about how to become more successful in life and business. Hopefully, my stuff helps people by offering some solid information, ideas, and opinions they can put to use.

Many of the memes out there are embarrassingly stupid and make no sense. They are not founded in logic. And they end up hurting people rather than helping people.

I saw one that said, "Nothing is impossible! Even the word itself says, 'I'm possible!'" Seriously? Yet the non-thinkers sit astride their unicorn and drool all over themselves to share this stupidity. If you are one of those who believe that nothing is impossible, try jumping off the Empire State Building and walking away from it. Try running a two-minute mile. Take your happy ass onto a basketball court and try to grab the rim of the basket when you're five-feet tall. Try to hold your breath underwater for 10 minutes. Should I go on? Lots of things are impossible. In fact, the definition of the word impossible is that it can't be done!

How about this one: "Never settle for less than you deserve." That sounds so brave, like it is about standing up for one's self, doesn't it? How could I possibly have an issue with that one? However, encouraging that mentality is one of our biggest societal issues. It gets people to focus on getting what they deserve instead of what they have earned. People already have an inflated case of deserved-ness, and we don't need to add to the problem. This is just more self-absorbed entitlement talk cloaked in personal development BS.

And this one: "Stay positive and you will always be happy" (insert smiley face). First, happiness does not come from being positive. Happiness can come from achieve-ment, being healthy, being satisfied, being alive, being content, from learning and growing, and a thousand other things. A hot fudge sundae can bring happiness. Second, how do you stay positive all the time? Do you not have a television? Do you not see what's going on in the world? How do you stay positive when horrible things are happening all around you? How do you stay positive when you lose someone close to you? We have created a society that wants to constantly shield itself from all things negative and from any and all unhappiness. It's impossible and detrimental to try. We have to understand that horrible things happen as a part of life and that it's completely natural to give in to the pain and feel it and even embrace it for a period of time. Constant euphoria exists only in a fantasy world, not the real world.

Here is another I saw posted, liked, and shared by thousands: "Everything you want is coming. Relax and let the universe pick the timing and the way. You just need to trust that what you want is coming, and watch how fast it comes" (Abraham Hicks).

Thanks, Abraham, for those laughable words of stupidity. We already have entire generations that are way too relaxed. They are waiting for what they want to show up. And what they are waiting for is typically a welfare check from the government that those of us who didn't wait paid for. Here's an idea: Stop waiting, stop being so relaxed, get off your lazy ass, and go earn what you want!

I love this one: "When you have a positive attitude you only see the positivity in the world around you." Not unless you live inside an M&M store. The world has plenty of negative in it and to ignore it is dumb. Where do these bozos come up with this stuff? Besides, a positive attitude doesn't keep negative things from happening in *the* world or in *your* world. In fact, I fully support having a negative attitude about many things. You can't create positive change in your life until you first get negative about your life. We don't change things when we feel good about them.

I saw this one just this morning: "Wake up every morning and say to yourself "I am the BEST!" Ridiculous. If you wake up and say, "I am the best" and make the mistake of believing it, you will never strive to get better. Instead of affirming what isn't true, work to make what you want to be true.

A guide for judging memes on social media:
If there is a rainbow, kitty, puppy, smiley face, sunrise or sunset, beach, or mountaintop in the background, chances are that the words in front of that picture are horseshit.

PEOPLE USE BAD GRAMMAR AND CAN'T SPELL

It is amazing how bad people's grammar has become. Most people seem to have completely missed elementary school (ironically called grammar school) where grammar was taught. Amazing they made it all the way through the education system yet never figured out the difference between their, they're, and there or you're and your. I blame teachers, I blame government, I blame the educational system, and I blame parents. However, at some point I blame the people who use the bad grammar. Personal responsibility does play a role here. At some point, you have to take the blame for the fact that you can't write a coherent sentence. You also have to realize that the point you are arguing for loses all credibility when you can't spell or use good grammar.

I recently posted this on my social media:

> "Your" shows possession. "You're" is a contraction for "you are." Saying "your an idiot" proves you're actually the idiot. Would you say "you're shoes"? Not unless you are a pair of shoes. Why is this so hard? Didn't you go to third grade?

As a result, people argued with me about how grammar doesn't matter any more. I find it nearly surreal that people can argue with me about this topic. What possible defense is there for using bad grammar? "I refused to learn anything in elementary school." Or how about, "I don't care about details like how to say things correctly"? Does that mean you also don't care about details like which financial plan you want me to invest in? Or what is really wrong with my car? Or about the house you want me to buy? Or how severe my cancer is? Details don't matter to you? Yet you want me to trust you with my money? My business? My health? My child's education? No thanks, I'll pass. If you use bad grammar, you are sending a message that makes everything you do subject to question. Can anyone really afford that loss of credibility in this highly competitive marketplace? I know I can't. But I also know that no one else can, either!

To further make my point about how ridiculous some in society have become about this issue: Mona Chalabi, a writer for *The Guardian*, says, "Grammar snobs are patronizing, pretentious, and just plain wrong." She goes on to say, "It doesn't take much to see the power imbalance when it comes to grammar snobbery. The people pointing out the mistakes are more likely to be older, wealthier, whiter, or just plain more academic than the people they're treating with condescension."

People can't spell, either. I blame Twitter in part for that. Ur for your, da for the, and other abbreviations have hindered our ability to spell. Then there is the problem of just not valuing the ability to spell to the point we would fail a kid in school for not being able to. There are also those who defend their inability to spell by pointing out all of the brilliant people in the world who haven't been able to spell, including William Faulkner, Ernest Hemingway, John Irving, Winston Churchill, and John F. Kennedy. Okay, I get that. I also get that you aren't those people. You need to know how to spell for all the same reasons you need to be able to use good grammar. Stop making excuses for your stupidity and learn how to spell.

A guy recently went after me on something I wrote on Facebook about using the made up word "tryna" instead of saying trying to. When I told him that I wasn't tryna to do anything, much less trying to, he called me a racist for making fun of his broken dialect. Seriously? Racist? Broken dialect? It took me three times to get the made-up word tryna to even post on Facebook since Facebook spell-check kept refusing to accept it and was changing it to trine. Why work so hard to use a stupid, made-up word and then defend it as broken dialect? Did this make his point more valid? No, it didn't. It only made him look stupid and caused him to call me a racist for pointing it out.

I also love the woman who disagreed with one of my posts and in blasting me, called me a moran. That's right: a *moran*. I replied back to her that her opinion of me showed a certain irony since I assumed she was calling me a moron but couldn't actually spell the word. She went nuts and said there was more than one way to spell it. When I asked her for proof of that, she said that different dictionaries spelled it different ways. I did my research of Webster, Oxford, Macmillan, and Cambridge as well as Dictionary.com and couldn't find any way to spell it except the correct way: m-o-r-o-n. Upon pointing this out to her, she quoted the Urban Dictionary to me. Do you have experience with the Urban Dictionary? It's a hoot. People submit their own definitions of words and some are hilarious. I pointed out to her that she should have read the definition supplied by the Urban Dictionary regarding the word moran. It says: "Moran, how a moron spells the word moron." Even after I pointed that out, she didn't back down.

Remember:

Spelchek is you're friend.
Their is know way to look smart to other's
when you right like an idiot.

PEOPLE LET THEIR EMOTIONS RULE THEIR LIVES

Before you get the idea that I am a nonemotional robot, rest assured that is far from the case. I am very emotional. I get angry; just ask my family and friends. I love completely.

I laugh more than anyone I know. Sometimes, I cry like a baby when something touches my heart like soldiers coming home, kids, and dogs. However, I don't cry over a cup of coffee or a plate of food that I feel compelled to post on Facebook. Though I did tear up a bit over some rib tips I ate in the cooking trailer of Myron Mixon, the Lord of Q.

There is a time and place for emotion.
But not every time and not every place.

People say, "Trust your gut." They also use "Listen to your heart." That's not always great advice. Your gut and your heart are both dumb as stumps. Don't believe me? Let's talk about your love life. I am betting you wish you could have many of the decisions back that you made by listening to your heart and when trusting your gut.

Instead, listen to your brain. Trust logic. Do what makes sense.

People who live in a constant state of emotion are typically not grounded and are easily distracted. They are constantly looking for what feeds their emotions. They also tend to be drama queens. Please don't think that drama queen is a description that only applies to females. I can show you lots of men who are drama queens as well.

Avoid people who live in a constant state of drama. These folks will suck you in and before you know it you are mired in their world of emotional chaos.

And while some live their lives based on emotions, some let emotions run their businesses as well.

Passion. The emotion I see that is most interfering with U.S. business today is the emotion of passion.

This one has bothered me for years. I go to meetings where they put up big screens with Steve Jobs and Tony Robbins quotes about the importance of passion. Hogwash.

Passion is defined as a barely controllable emotion. Look it up. I don't want a barely controllable emotion anywhere near my business. You don't, either. And if you do want to run your life and business by an emotion, why pick passion? Why not anger? Why not rage? Why not silliness? Why not grief or sadness? One emotion is about as good as the next, isn't it?

Still not convinced? I know you aren't, by the way. You passionate people will cling to your passion and the need for it like a drowning man in the middle of the ocean clings to his life vest. So answer this question for me:

You need quadruple bypass surgery. The hospital brings you two cardiologists. One is passionate about cutting people open. It excites him. He can't wait to do it every day. He loves it. It is his reason for being. The other works hard every day to be the best cardiologist he can be. He is focused on excellence. He does constant research to make sure he is at the top of his game. He constantly assesses his successes and his failures to make sure he improves every time he does surgery. He hates cutting people open, but when necessary, he knows he is totally prepared to do so with good results. Tell me, which surgeon do you want?

Thought so.

So let's set aside all of the Pollyanna ideas and go back to what works and what makes sense every single time: knowledge, research, logic, and common sense. Set emotion aside for your family and friends and let your brain run your business.

PEOPLE FOLLOW THEIR DREAMS
INSTEAD OF GOING TO WORK

Not a week goes by that someone doesn't contact me telling me how they hate their job and are tired of working to make the other guy rich, and they're ready to follow their dream and start their own business. In fact, a recent poll says that 55 percent of millennials want to go into business for themselves. I admire people who have that entrepreneurial spirit and want to take control of their future.

Very few people will actually start their own business. It is a dream that will never become a reality for most. Why? Laziness. Most folks are great at dreaming about what they want, but when it comes to putting their butt into gear and actually doing the work, they sit down and turn the television back on and realize that job they have where the check shows up every other Friday isn't so bad after all. So the years go by and nothing in their life changes.

STARTING YOUR OWN BUSINESS IS
NOT A DREAM, IT'S A NIGHTMARE

When I respond to people about going into business for themselves, people think I am a downer because I am rarely encouraging. Maybe it is because I know the stats on how few of them will succeed. I know because I can read, use a search engine, and am a realist. I know that, depending on whose research you want to go with, some-where between 33 and 50 percent of new businesses fail in the first two years and somewhere between 60 and 90 percent are history in five years. And don't say, "Yeah, but I won't be one of them!" Really? They all said that. None of them said, "I am going to invest all of my time, money, and energy into a business that will probably be out of business in 24 months and will almost definitely be out of business in five years." So let me ask you, Why won't you? What makes you the exception? Wait! Don't answer yet—keep reading before you answer and embarrass yourself.

WHY DO MOST BUSINESSES FAIL?
LACK OF PREPARATION

Answer these questions:

- Do you have real-world, hands-on experience running a business?
- Have you read a book on how to start a business?
- Have you taken a course on marketing and advertising?
- Do you know how to hire, fire, train, and manage people?
- Are you undercapitalized? Do you even know what that means?
- Do you know what a balance sheet is and how to read one?
- Do you have a realistic view of what your expenses will be? (Hint: double that number.)

- Do you know what your breakeven is, and do you have a plan for what you are going to do when you are short and what you are going to do with the profits?
- Do you know the survival rate of businesses in your industry?
- Do you know the importance of customer service and how to deliver it?
- Do you know how to sell?
- Do you know what differentiates you from your competitors?
- Do you even know if there is a need or market for your product or service? Are you sure? Before you answer that one, what analysis have you done? Just because your BFF and your sister-in-law said they would buy from you, it doesn't mean there is a need or a real market.

Or are you opening your business based on your passion for what you do or your desire to be your own boss? If that is your delusion, you will soon be disappointed. And you will be broke and discouraged and right back where you started, only in much worse shape. Wiser but broker.

Open a business because you provide a needed service and because you solve a problem, and then only do it when you are prepared. Don't let passion, that barely controllable emotion, be your guide. Logic, money, research, skills, preparedness, and market need should instead be your determining factors.

And be clear about this: Regardless of what some coaches and multilevel marketing (MLM) companies might tell you, some people are not meant to be in business for themselves. Not everyone is cut out to be an entrepreneur. In fact, ask the MLM folks to show you the stats on how many that start actually stay, and of those who stay, how many make real money. MLM is like everything else; it looks great from the outside but the reality is, very few make any real money. Sooner, rather than later, you will run out of friends to sell to. Then what will you do? Spam people's newsfeeds on Facebook? That is your marketing plan?

Robert Kiyosaki, author of *Rich Dad, Poor Dad*, said in a *TIME* interview, "Most people are wimps, pussies, cowards—they should get a job."

He also says in several interviews and online videos that jobs are for losers and that paychecks are evil.

Of course, Kiyosaki was more than likely just trying to get you to invest in his program so he could have more of your money and you would have less of your money—money you got from your paycheck while working at . . . wait for it . . . a job!

His comments are some of the most insulting to working men and women I have ever heard. They are demeaning to every person who shows up, puts in their hours, and earns a paycheck. And they are dead wrong.

Jobs are not for wimps, pussies, and cowards. People with jobs are not losers. Paychecks are not evil. Jobs are for people who want to work to earn money so they can pay their bills and take care of their families. Jobs are the fabric of our economy. Jobs will fix damn near every issue we have in our society as well. So never demean or let anyone of these entrepreneurial bozos demean having a job. When you hear these elitist hacks say that J.O.B. stands for Just

Over Broke (thanks again, Robert Kiyosaki), you need to know that is also an insult to hard-working men and women all over the world and that jobs are what keep people from being totally broke. Every job has dignity.

Don't let these pathetic asshats toy with your emotions to the point you believe that you need to become an entrepreneur to establish your self-worth or to create wealth. It's a lie! Besides, most people should *never* become entrepreneurs!

Some people are much better off having a job and working for someone who knows how to run a profitable business. That is nothing to be ashamed of but something to be very proud of. I am sick of the concept that working for someone else is "settling for a job when you could be living your dream of living life on your own terms." No one who does make it as an entrepreneur will tell you they live life on their own terms. To be successful in your own business, you will live your life on the terms of your banker, your suppliers, your employees, your customers, the government, and the economy.

All of the entrepreneurial coaches need a dose of reality before they tell people to quit their day job and to become an entrepreneur. Usually that is the worst advice you can give someone. Most people want and need a job. They need that stability. They claim they want freedom but there is much more freedom in working for someone else than in owning your own business. If you are that person (and most are) who is happy to go to work and do your job, then be thankful that you have one, and give it your best every day. Few things are more honorable.

Finally, before you think about going into business I want you to answer in detail and on paper each of the questions I asked above. I want you to examine yourself and your skills. I want you to be brutally honest with yourself about your motives. I want you to know the value you bring to the marketplace and to actually know the marketplace. And I want you to remember the words of Dirty Harry: "A good man knows his limitations."

Now, after reading this, answer the question I asked earlier: "Why won't you go out of business like the majority of people do? What makes you different? How prepared are you?"

PEOPLE ARE ENTITLED

I said in my last book, *Grow a Pair*, that entitlement mentality will ultimately be what destroys our country. While I still believe that, it is imperative that we understand that entitlement mentality is just a symptom and not the cause of our problems. The cause is that we no longer teach and practice self-sufficiency as a core value. And we don't expect it or demand it from every member of our family and from society.

Entitlement breeds laziness, which in turn breeds decline.

From The Short Drop *by Matthew FitzSimmons*

I was taught to be self-sufficient by my parents. Growing up, there was never a time when I was allowed to think that I wasn't totally responsible for taking care of myself physically, financially, and emotionally. I was taught to never expect anything to be done for me by anyone. Therefore, it has never crossed my mind to rely on others, especially the government, to support me in any way.

As a kid, when someone hurt my feelings, I was expected to get over it and move on. I was taught that the other person was the one with the problem, not me. I was reminded constantly of the old saying, "Sticks and stones may break my bones but words will never hurt me."

When I was bullied, I was expected to stand up and fight for myself. My dad taught me that it was better to nurse a bloody nose than to lose my dignity. I was also taught to never pick on anyone for any reason. I wasn't allowed to look down on others because they weren't like me. What color you were didn't matter. How much money you had didn't matter. Since we didn't have any money, we certainly didn't put others down for not having money. But we didn't put down folks for having a lot of money, either. I was taught to respect people for who they were, not what they were or what they had.

If I needed something done, I was taught to do it. I didn't expect anyone else to do it for me. And I didn't ask for help doing it until I had tried my best all by myself.

If I wanted something, I was expected to figure out a way to get it on my own. That usually meant that I would walk the highway with a tow sack (a burlap feed sack) filling it with pop bottles I could later sell for two cents apiece. I would pick strawberries and go door-to-door selling them. I didn't get an allowance and I didn't get paid for chores, of which there were plenty. Chores were my obligation to helping out the family. I earned money from other people, not my parents. And when working for other people I was taught to show up early, do more than expected, to work hard while I was there, and to be appreciative of the opportunity. Does that sound similar to much of what I am saying in this book? I hope so. Those core values were instilled in me as a child.

Notice how often in what I just wrote about my childhood that I used the word *expect*. There was an expectation engrained in me by my parents. That expectation was that I was responsible for myself in every way.

Very few parents teach much of this today. For the most part, children learn to expect that someone will always be there to take care of them. And that, folks, is how you end up with the most entitled generation in history. A recent Pew Research Poll discovered that 43 percent of 18- to 29-year-olds prefer socialism to capitalism. Thirty-two percent prefer a government-managed economy to a free-market economy. Go ahead, pause and shake your head in disgust.

We even have millennials who bring their parents to job interviews with them. Many even ask if it is okay for their parents to negotiate their salary for them. Do you want to hire an employee who needs a babysitter? I don't. I can't imagine a manager or owner interviewing a person whose parents are sitting right there with them. In fact, I would refuse to do the interview at the instant Mom and Dad walked in; I would know everything I needed to know. I hire adults, not children. Is this the kid's fault? Of course it is. But the bulk of the blame still goes to the parent for not teaching the kid (now an adult) to be self-sufficient. By the way, this is a prime example of helicopter parenting.

ENTITLEMENT IS THE ENEMY OF SELF-RELIANCE

I was taught at home, at school, and at church that if I got an education, worked hard, treated people right, and was smart with my money that I could be successful. That concept was reinforced by society. Now we have too many people who believe that if I do that, they have the right to take that from me because they are owed a part of my money simply because they aren't willing to do the same things I have done. They don't have that core value of self-sufficiency. They believe that we should all share equally regardless of who does the work and earns the money.

This does not mean that I don't believe we should help others. I do. However, I do not believe in taking care of others. Instead, I believe in teaching people to take care of themselves. However, this can only be done if people believe they should take care of themselves. Which means a shift in what we are teaching our kids and what we expect and demand from them.

If you teach your children they should expect free college, free health care, free food, and free money instead of working to earn those things for themselves, you have done your children a huge disservice. If they have been taught to believe any of those things are "rights," then you have misled them. Those things should all be earned. None of those are something you are entitled to.

If you are not teaching your children what my parents taught me and others of my generation—to get an education, work hard, treat people right, and be smart with your money—then in my book you are a lousy parent. And if you think I am saying that my generation was right and that the younger generation is wrong when it comes to teaching, learning, and living these core values, that is exactly what I am saying. The evidence is everywhere.

Stopping entitlement mentality doesn't start in the White House, it starts in *your* house.

It's obvious that parents are not teaching their kids how to be self-sufficient when you have 36 percent of millennials living with their parents.

Parents, is this what you had in mind for your adult children when they were born? Did you look at that sweet, innocent, tiny, little baby and hope he would reach adulthood and still live in his bedroom well into his 30s? If you did, you are a horrible parent. And if your adult children live with you now, you are still a bad parent. I have heard every excuse in the world. "They fell on hard times." "It's perfectly acceptable in other cultures." "We love having them here and helping them." "We are one big, happy family." All excuses. Here is the truth: If you don't equip your children with the skills to survive and thrive on their own and achieve independence, you are an abusive parent. You don't love your kids. You are enablers who are selfish and delusional. You are a failure as a parent.

Plus, you are stupid. You are sacrificing your financial future—possibly your retirement—all because you don't have the balls to do what you should have done a long time ago: kick their lazy asses out!

THE GOVERNMENT IS FEEDING ENTITLEMENT MENTALITY

Didn't take care of yourself? Bought a house you couldn't afford and can't pay for? No money for food because you spent it all on drugs and booze? Can't afford to go to college? Too lazy to work or look for a job? Irresponsibly had too many kids and can't take care of them? Sad or depressed and need some government money to feel better?

This list is just the beginning, and you know it. If you have a problem, the government will be right there to solve it for you.

Now there is not only a willingness of people to be taken care of by the hard work of others, there is a sense of entitlement that they deserve to be taken care of by others. In fact, we encourage it. Go on your Facebook newsfeed and look at the ads paid for by the government suggesting that people are likely due more from the government than they would have ever thought. Ads suggesting that they contact the Social Security Administration. There is even an ad suggesting to Americans that they can get money from Canada without ever having worked there or lived there. And it tries to ease your conscience by saying, don't worry, you aren't taking money from the Canadian government but from private businesses in Canada. It has testimonials from proud Americans who admit they are getting thousands of dollars from Canada after having done nothing to earn it. People laugh at screwing over others to get ahead, thinking that as long as it doesn't cost them anything, it's justified. Some think actions like this don't cost real people, only governments and businesses. Any idea where the government gets the money to pay freeloaders? Or how businesses earn the money that pays for this stuff? Ever think it through that every time you scam a business, it makes it up by charging its customers more?

Bernie Sanders, during his run in the 2016 presidential race, appealed to people with a high deservedness factor. The group with the highest "I deserve stuff" score is millennials. Of course, millennials aren't the only ones who have an entitlement mentality, for sure. There are many low-wage earners who believe they deserve to be paid more even though their value in the marketplace is low.

There is something called the Universal Law of Sowing and Reaping, which teaches that you reap what you sow. Entitlement mentality is all about reaping without sowing. No effort at all still gets you a reward. This flies in the face of what makes sense to the rest of us: rewards only come *after* effort.

So after years of learning in school and at home that you should expect to be rewarded for little or no effort, many young voters are of the mind that that should carry on throughout their entire lives. That's why free college, free health care, expansion of Social Security, growth of entitlement programs and welfare programs—in other words, complete government dependence from the cradle to the grave—is very appealing to them.

They want a government that will do things for them while the rest of us want a government that will get out of the way so we can do things for ourselves.

This is a shame because parents didn't take the time to teach them that everything carries a cost—and I'm not talking about everything having a price. I'm talking about a cost. I honestly believe that if the entitled were educated about the cost of everything and asked how it can all be paid for, then they would see things differently.

In case you still aren't clear on this one, just remember this: You are entitled to nothing except your own opinion.

"But, but, but, but . . ."

Save it. Offering any argument to this statement is just one more step toward victimhood.

No one owes you anything, and the faster you grasp that thought and begin to own it, the freer you will be. When you stop expecting anyone—from the government, to your boss, to your spouse or parents or friends—to take care of you, you will finally start to experience your own personal power.

The problem with the government being so open and so willing to take care of people is that it creates government dependency and destroys self-sufficiency.

We claim we want a government that gives us independence and freedom, yet what we have really created is a government that steals our freedoms and encourages dependence.

We have politicians who run on the platform of giving people more free stuff. Great platform for getting elected in a society where there are more people on the government teat than ever before. The takers now outnumber the makers. Just promise people more free stuff and they will line up in droves to support you—especially since they don't have jobs to keep them from doing so.

When there is an expectation that someone else should or will take care of you, there is no need to bother taking care of yourself.

It's why we have sixth-generation welfare recipients. We literally breed dependency. It's also why some people would rather collect unemployment than get a job.

Self-reliance is becoming a thing of the past. What our government is teaching people to expect is government reliance. The Declaration of Independence has been converted to a Declaration of Government Dependence.

The other thing that this entitlement mentality encourages is that when you can't get the free stuff you think you are entitled to, then you have the right to take it. Entitlement mentality grows into a criminal mentality.

Welfare fraud is everywhere and it costs Americans about $60 billion dollars per year.

President Lyndon Johnson declared a war on poverty in 1964. We have lost that war. And the defeat becomes more profoundly evident every year.

- According to the U.S. Census Bureau, 49.2 percent of Americans receive benefits from one or more government programs.
- According to Health and Human Services, 23.1 percent of Americans are receiving benefits from one of the three major welfare programs.
- There are nearly 47 million people receiving food stamps.
- Welfare spending is on the rise.

Welfare was intended to be a temporary assistance program—a Band-Aid—but it has become a crutch. If you take a stand against it, as I have here, you will be called uncaring and told you lack compassion. I disagree. Welfare programs make people more dependent on the government and less dependent on themselves. It is not compassionate to undermine self-sufficiency; it is abuse.

Here are my ideas about what to do about welfare programs:

- Welfare and food stamps are *not* the answer. There are better answers that will have a real, long-lasting effect.
- Wean people off of government assistance.
- Jerk the rug out from under able-bodied men and women with no dependents.
- Demand that government reduce the number of people on welfare and food stamps and the amount it spends on these programs.
- Demand that government create a climate of job growth.
- Teach job skills and financial literacy in our public school systems so people are prepared to take a job and earn their own way.
- Communicate to the citizens that jobs—not government programs—are the answer to poverty.
- Tell people they will be expected to take care of themselves and not to rely on the government to take care of them.
- Jobs are the answer. Education is the answer. Communicating higher expectations is the answer.

If we want to reverse our course as a nation, we must teach people to go back to that list of words that have the root word of "self": Self-sufficiency. Self-respect. Self-reliance. Self-confidence. All of those things come when people are employed; they do not come from getting a government check.

PEOPLE ARE FULL OF EXCUSES AND BLAME

I preach personal responsibility for a living. I have written books with titles like *Shut Up, Stop Whining and Get a Life*; *Your Kids Are Your Own Fault*; and *You're Broke Because You Want to Be* that are obviously about telling people that their situations are their responsibility. My mantra and the basis for all I do is, "Your life is your own damn fault!"

Spend over 25 years doing that for a living, write six bestsellers that say that, stand on thousands of stages around the world speaking about how to do that in your life and business, and go on television regularly saying that and trust me, you are going to be bombarded with excuses. Try it yourself: Go tell someone what they can do in their life to be better and 9 times out of 10 you will hear all of the reasons they can't do it. They are too old or too young. They are white, black, or brown. They will tell you they don't have any money. Then they will talk about their education or how they were raised or that they were the middle child. People are desperate to find an excuse for why any idea that involves taking action can't be done and won't work for them.

These people call them reasons. To be clear, what people call reasons are rarely anything more than excuses.

That's right. Your reason is your excuse. How do I know that? Because I can show you too many examples of who defied the odds and did what they set out to do anyway. Nothing stood in their way.

So get this straight: If you aren't going to do it, just tell yourself that you don't have what it takes to do it. Tell yourself you are a loser who isn't willing to do the work. Then convince yourself that being successful, happy, and financially secure in loving relationships doesn't matter. Be honest with yourself and everyone else and just say, "I don't want to, I'm satisfied with the mess I have created, and I'm not willing to do anything to change it." But please, don't offer us your worthless words that you have sold yourself on as legitimate reasons for living the life you live. We don't want to hear them. Everyone who has made anything of their life or business or relationships knows that if you want it badly enough, you will do whatever it takes to make it happen. They know that words don't mean diddly-squat. They know that if you want to, you will, and if you don't, it's because you really didn't want to. That's the way it works.

Spend as much time and energy finding a solution as you do on finding an excuse, and your problems will go away much quicker.

"But, but, but Larry! You don't understand! My boss . . ." or "my husband . . ." or "my kids . . ." or "my bank . . ." Hey, there's always something.

We all have crap we have to deal with. We all have problems. If you think your problems are unique or tougher than someone else's, then let me open your eyes to reality: No matter how big your problem is, someone has a bigger one. And they deal with it. And they conquer it. And their problem doesn't become their excuse for a "less than" life.

Remember this:

Your success lies somewhere between
what you will do and what you aren't willing to do.

If you are willing to do whatever it takes to get and
have what you want, there is a pretty high likelihood that
you will achieve it. It takes work. It takes action. It takes
making yourself break a sweat.

Stop saying you can't. It's not that you can't, it's that
you won't or don't want to.

Make a list of everything that's holding you back.
It won't take long, just write "*me*."

PEOPLE ARE DISHONEST AND LACK INTEGRITY

1,625,000. What does that number represent? According
to Statisticbrain.com, it's the number of people who cheat
on their taxes each year. Now I'm meddling, right? After
all, what does a little fudging here and there on the home
office deduction or the charitable expenses really matter,
anyway? Not much I guess, given that it only costs the
United States $270,000,000,000 every year.

According to a University of Massachusetts study,
60 percent of us can't go more than 10 minutes without
lying.

A survey from Careerbuilder.com says that 58 percent
of hiring managers have caught job applicants in a lie. Of
the lies, 57 percent relate to embellished skill sets, and

26 percent are people saying that they worked for a company they never actually worked for.

According to moneycrashers.com, 31 percent of women and 27 percent of men admit to lying to their spouses about money. In fact, financial infidelity is one of the top issues between spouses.

But these are big things right? Okay, let's look at the little white lies people tell. According to ranker.com, these are the things people lie about most often.

- I'm fine.
- I'm five minutes away.
- Let's keep in touch.
- My phone died.
- I've got to go.
- I'm busy that day.
- I'm listening.
- I forgot.
- I love it!
- I got caught in traffic.

Do any of these sound familiar to you? Sure they do. Face it; you're a liar.

Jimmy Kimmel does a bit on his show, *Jimmy Kimmel Live*, called "Lie Witness News," where people will lie about movies they haven't seen, what they saw and heard in the State of the Union address when they clearly didn't see it, and various other things in the news that are obviously made up and more. Why do they lie? Because they don't want to appear to be stupid or uninformed, so they make it up. While the bit is hilarious, it's also really scary.

My dad always told me, "Some people will lie when it's easier to tell the truth." I have learned that he was absolutely right.

Larry's Number One Rule for Life and Business
Do what you said you would do,
when you said you would do it,
the way you said you would do it.

That line has appeared in all of my other books. I happily repeat it here because I believe that line represents most of what it takes to be successful. It is a line based on the core values of honesty and integrity. It states exactly what your customers want from you. It's what you want from your employees. It's what your employees want from you and you from your employees. It's what you want from our politicians and from your garbage collector. It's what you want from your spouse or your partner and your kids. And it's exactly what they want from you as well.

Let me follow that thought all the way through: If you *don't* do what you said you would, when you said you would do it, the way you said you would do it, you are a liar. That's right, you are a liar. It's that simple. It's that black and white. You are a liar when you tell your wife you will take out the trash and you don't do it. You are a liar when you tell your kids you will play with them and then plop your butt in front of the television instead. You are a liar when you tell your customer you will call them at 10:00 and you don't get around to it until 10:20. And you are a liar when you are late to work.

When you sign a contract with a credit card company to pay your bill on the 15th of the month and you pay the bill after that, you are a liar. No two ways about it: you said you would and you didn't.

When you tell your child, "If you do that again, I am going to ground you," and then they do it again and you don't ground them, you are a lying parent. Is that something you want to teach your kids? That your word can't be trusted? That it's okay to lie? Your example just taught them that.

"Oh come on, Larry! I'm not a liar, it's just that something came up and I didn't get to it as quickly as I said I would." You're right, I understand completely how that could happen. And you're still a liar.

If you said you would do it and you didn't do it, regardless of why you didn't do it, you still didn't do it. That means you lied. Paint it pink and put a bow on it all you want to. Do what it takes to make yourself feel better about it. Tell yourself whatever you need to. But be clear, if you didn't keep your word, you lied. You weren't honest.

WE HAVE BECOME WAY TOO TOLERANT OF DISHONESTY

People vote for candidates who are known liars and crooks because they value what those candidates can do for them personally more than they do the candidates' honesty in all matters. It's more important for them to cater to your desires or interests than it is for them to be truthful.

I recently had a person argue with me that her candidate stretches the truth but that doesn't really make the person a liar. It's that kind of thinking that proves my point regarding the collapse of core values. If a politician's lies support our selfish desires then we water them down and call it stretching the truth.

Promise to double the minimum wage and the people who are on minimum wage will show up to vote for you. Promise to take care of the rich and the rich will vote for you. It doesn't matter whether the person doing the promising has been proven to be a liar or if we know he is dishonest. If we can benefit in some way personally, then we will happily sell out our values in order to do so. Which means those values weren't all that valuable to us in the first place.

The two presidential candidates in 2016 were both liars. No two ways about it, they both lied to the American people on numerous occasions about some very serious matters. And the bottom line is that their core supporters simply didn't care. Their dishonesty didn't matter to their respective bases. To be clear, if you vote for people you know are dishonest, then don't claim that honesty matters to you, because it doesn't. And while it is a damn shame to have political candidates who are dishonest, it's a horrible personal shame that we, as a society, have allowed them to rise to this level. I care more about that issue than the fact that our candidates are liars.

Until we teach the core value of being honest and practice it in every aspect of our own lives, then demand it from everyone we are associated with and stop tolerating it at any level, we can expect to keep getting more of what we've got.

Self-interest has become our moral compass in determining what is honest and what it dishonest.

Want another example about how subtle dishonesty is slipping into our culture? IKEA has a commercial where a woman paying for her merchandise at the register looks at her receipt and is so surprised by how low it is that she assumes that they have made a mistake on the price. In real life, an honest person would have stopped and questioned whether the price was right in an effort to assure she was paying the correct amount for what she was buying. However, in the commercial she runs out of the store, hops in the car with her husband, and tells him to *drive*!!! In other words, she thinks the store has made an error in her favor and she wants to steal that amount from the store, get something for nothing, and run away before getting caught. She is perfectly fine with stealing from the store. In reality she just got a good deal and that is the point of the commercial, but the message is that when someone makes a mistake in your favor, run before you get caught. What message is that sending our children? That it's okay to steal and funny when you screw over a company for making a mistake in your favor.

People lack integrity. Recently, one of my close friends and one of the foremost leadership speakers in the United States, had another speaker use his name and material to promote himself on Facebook. This happens a lot. I have seen my own face used to promote others people's programs. People I have never heard of. I always take swift action when this happens to me and I speak up when I see it happening to someone else. It is degrading to my industry, one that should be built on honesty and integrity. But this one also riled me up because it was taking advantage of and hurting my friend. I'm one of those guys who believes that when you see injustice, you speak up, and when someone attacks your friend, you're the first one in the fight to help.

I went on the guy's Facebook page and pointed out how unethical what he had just done was and that it was a reflection of his character to steal another's material and to capitalize on the reputation of someone at a much higher level. Several of our mutual friends did the same. This guy's response to me was: "My job is not to make friends but to win. I will use every legal stratagem to defeat my competitors." Here is a guy who teaches people how to become leaders, proudly saying that it doesn't matter if what he is doing is ethical, because as long as it is legal and he benefits from it, he will continue to do it. Is this a guy you want teaching our leaders? Yet, he has a following that will support him because honesty and integrity aren't core values to them. Only winning is of value to them. Winning is not a core value.

To win at any cost is to lose.

Role Models. Role models are nothing more than a reflection of what we value. When we value honesty, integrity, doing the right thing, morals, good parenting, leadership, and hard work, we will have role models who exemplify those values. Since we instead value fame, celebrity, being pretty, and living an ostentatious lifestyle, we find ourselves with role models that conform to those values.

Let me give you a prime example of the stupidity of some of these folks:

> Some people write novels and they just be so wordy and self-absorbed. I am not a fan of books. I would never want a book's autograph. I am a proud nonreader of books.
>
> **—Kanye West**

When you, as a parent, see something like this, use it as a teaching moment to point out how sad a statement like this is. Point out that people who say things like this are ignorant on many levels. Don't allow your children to believe that a guy like this should be admired. Do the same when you see a sports figure do something abhorrent like beat his wife or girlfriend or get caught using drugs. Don't allow your kids to look up to these asshats.

When we elevate our values we will elevate our role models. It's fine to admire what people accomplish in business, sports, or the financial world, but it's stupid to turn them into role models unless they are the kind of people you want your child to grow up to be. For instance: Steve Jobs quotes are posted on social media every day as if he was a guru of business, yet he screwed over his partners. Tiger Woods is the greatest golfer who ever lived but he is not a good guy. Before we hold any person up as a role model, we need to look at more than what he does, what he has, and how he looks. We must look at who they are and how they live.

Because of the collapse of the core values of kindness, charity, love, being nice, and respect, people resort to meanness as a way of dealing with each other.

PEOPLE ARE MEAN

I sometimes am accused of being mean. That characterization disappoints me. I'm direct. I am opinionated. I am sarcastic and sometimes caustic. I am politically incorrect, but I am not mean. We have reached a place where being direct is considered mean. But I'm not talking about being direct; I am talking about true meanness.

It is not mean to attack behavior or results, especially when you are paying for those results. It is mean to attack people.

There are many reasons for meanness.

The Internet is one of the biggest reasons for meanness. Anonymity. You can respond to a post on social media with no repercussions at all. When a lack of accountability and consequences exist, behavior goes awry. In too many cases, people say things to each other on the Internet that they would never have the balls to say face to face.

I rarely comment on someone else's thread on any social media platform. But when I do, I make sure that my comment adds to the thread and doesn't hijack it and force it to go in another direction. I am cognizant of the fact that it is not my thread or my page and I respect the owner's position and am only there to add to the conversation, never detract from it. I never want someone else's thread to become about me, and I never mention my products or services in any way because it's not my thread to advertise on. I know that unless I see my name and picture at the top of the page, that I am a guest. I treat other people's pages and posts with the same respect I would treat their houses. And while I would disagree with them in their house, I would do it respectfully, and I wouldn't take a crap in the corner for sure. This position is firmly based in the core values of respect and kindness.

BUSINESS HAS BECOME MEAN

Meanness has become a whole language in the business world as well. It has also become a personal development cult. There are success gurus who sell domination and destruction as the path to wealth. They insist that you be obsessed with crushing it and destroying the competition and say that to become a true champion you have to dominate! One of them even says that unless you are obsessed with thinking this way, you are a "little bitch." His words, not mine.

I recently took a stand against some particularly bad financial advice one of these gurus gave about investing. I never mentioned his name, just addressed his advice. He was made aware of it and suggested to his million-plus followers that they come on my page and comment to defend his way of thinking. And comment they did, with vitriolic name-calling like I have never experienced. I deleted their comments, of course, as I refuse to be disrespected, especially on my own page. However, I learned a lot about the mentality of meanness from this experience. Selling people on the ideas of obsession, domination, and destruction in business carries over to the way you deal with others on a personal level. I came to pity the lemmings that follow the success gurus who preach this philosophy. They fail to understand that success in business and life is based on service to others, adding value to every situation, and treating people with respect even when you disagree with them. A mentality of making others succumb to your dominance leaves no winners in any type of relationship. Yes, it will work for a while and people who whole-heartedly embrace this thinking will appear to be winning, but I believe that in the long run, these people will come out losers. Instead of a mean-spirited approach to business (which spills over into life) where you are obsessed with dominating, destroying, and crushing it, take a deep breath and consider how you can improve the situation, add value, solve a problem where both parties feel good about the exchange, and serve others well with your product, service, and attitude. Do that and you will have long-term success and satisfaction you can take to the grave with pride.

We have reached the point where we confuse meanness with being competitive when being competitive should be based on simply being better than others you compete against.

The solution? I suggest that to counteract all of this meanness we try a little kindness.

There are great acts of kindness going on in the world for sure. And I don't discount them in any way. But random acts of kindness have become too random. Kindness should be predictable.

Sometimes it is kinder when you hear something ridiculously stupid to just let it slide. This is a hard one for me. I know it's hard for many of you, too. I have a lot of stupid things said to me (you do, too, I know), and when I hear them or read them, I am prone to cut someone off at the knees. It's easy for me to do that—I'm good at it. I have to remind myself to be kind and let some things slide, mostly because I know that nothing would change as a result of my speaking up.

Conversely, sometimes the kind thing to do is to speak up and address the issue head on. Sometimes it is actually kind to cut someone off at the knees. How do you know when to and when not to? When speaking up does make a difference, then I believe you are obligated to do so. When your words or actions could change the situation to make things better, then don't pass up the opportunity to make the situation better.

Speaking of kindness, let's start practicing it with people who are different from us. There is no excuse to be unkind to people based on their being black or white, gay or straight, or because they believe differently than you do about God or whether they even believe in God. Please disagree with them if you don't believe as they do. That's fine and can create more understanding. But disagreement should never be unkind.

In a society where meanness rules,
kindness gets harder to find.
Yet it's never hard to perform.

PEOPLE ARE LAZY

This one is easy to prove. I could do it by quoting how many hours per day people spend watching television (more than five hours per day). Or how much of their time on the job is not spent doing the job but screwing off (up to three hours per day). Or how much time is spent on their device (nine hours per day). I could even cite that now many businesses are now allowing naptime on the job because their employees get tired in the mornings and afternoons, and a little nap on company time makes them more productive. Instead, I want to go after all of those people who are perfectly capable of getting a job and working, yet have decided not to participate in the job market.

When I was young and broke, I did whatever it took to get employed. Why? I wanted stuff. And that's the difference between then and now. No one gave me anything. My mom and dad were doing all they could to pay their own bills. They flat out didn't have the money to give me all of the stuff I wanted. And if they would have had unlimited funds, they still wouldn't have given me all of the stuff I wanted. They would have done just what they did: taught me to work for what I wanted.

We have lots of mamas and daddies today who also can't afford to give stuff to their kids, but they are sacrificing their retirement and all they have to give it to their grown, adult kids. That's wrong. It's wrong for the parents who feel they should or feel they have to and it's wrong for the kids to take it. I went door to door to businesses in Muskogee, Oklahoma, asking for a job. I was willing to do anything. And I mean *anything* that was moral and legal.

Too many people are too damn picky. They only want a job that fits with their life purpose. What the hell is that, anyway? How do you know what your life purpose even is at 20 years old? I didn't figure out what my life purpose was until after I had a job for more than 20 years. These silly folks want to follow their bliss or find their passion. Me? I didn't care about any of those things. I just wanted a damn job! Why? Again, it's all because I wanted stuff. I needed stuff. I needed a job that would pay me so I could get some stuff. Let's be clear: People still want stuff. There are jobs that will pay them so they can get stuff. But when people give you stuff or give you money or a government program or even several government programs so you never have to earn any money to get stuff, then there is no reason to get a job and work for a living.

Mamas and daddies . . . stop giving your lazy-ass kids stuff and stop giving them money. Government . . . stop giving lazy-ass people stuff and stop giving them money. Stop making it easier for people *not* to get a job by creating one more government program that the rest of us who do have jobs have to pay for. Everyone: Stop being lazy, go find a job—whether you like the job or not—and earn money to buy your own stuff.

Work and work hard—it's what you are paid to do! There was a time when we not only valued our own ability to go out and create a great life through hard work, but we had the desire to work. Now we don't value the desire and we value sitting on our ass and pride ourselves in collecting a government check and laughing about how our unemployment checks are higher than minimum wage, so why not?

Most people are cursed with a combination of too much *want* and too much *won't*.

You probably don't have what you want in life because you weren't willing to work hard enough to get it. Am I saying that you're lazy? Probably. The statistics to back me up on that are pretty strong. However, maybe you aren't lazy and you genuinely work hard and your hard work isn't yielding many rewards. Then it comes down to this: you are lying to yourself. This happens a lot. Very few people honestly understand how hard they work or don't work. They know they are busy and equate busyness with work.

Work is the accomplishment of a task. It's not what you do; it's what you get done.

Work solves most problems. When you are faced with a problem, you can almost always work your way out of that problem. Now I know many of you will disagree with that concept and can argue it quite convincingly. It's not important to me that you agree with that idea or not, but you will have to agree with the concept that even if you can't work your way out of all problems, whining, complaining, blaming, and playing the victim never solves a problem.

When I was a kid I made the decision that I would get rich. I didn't have a clue how to do it but I knew this: I knew I could outwork everyone. I might not be better than them or have as many skills as they had, but I could start earlier, stay later, hustle a little more, smile a little more, complain a little less, and stick with a task no matter how difficult it was in order to be better than anyone else. I could flat out outwork anyone.

When I made the decision to become a professional speaker I followed that same line of thinking. I may not have had any more talent than others in the business, but I knew I could outwork everyone in the business to make it to the top. And that's what I set about doing. I made more calls and read more books and gave more bad speeches so I could learn how to do it better the next time. I worked hard to become the Larry Winget whose book you are reading right now.

When the going gets tough, the weak typically whine, blame, beg for help, or quit—while the strong focus, buckle down, work harder, and get it done.

PEOPLE ARE DISRESPECTFUL AND UNCIVIL

Chances are very high that you and I don't agree on many things. I can say that without having ever met you. And that's not about me and it's not about you. It's about people. I don't agree with how most people drive, or raise their kids, or spend their money. I don't agree with the way many people vote. The list of what I don't agree with that people do is long.

However, while I will adamantly disagree with those things and happily speak my mind about it, I won't be disrespectful to you for believing differently than I do.

I won't attack you. I will, however, attack your beliefs, your words, and your actions. Please feel free to do the same with me. Just be respectful while you do it.

That proposition seems to be more than fair. We don't do that much any more. We have stopped disagreeing and started disrespecting.

I would never think of saying some of what is said to people by others today. Especially, to people in positions of authority or people who are older. I am certainly not saying that people who are older or in positions of authority are always right, but their position and age merit respect.

I still say yes sir and no ma'am and give people older than I am respect. Their age demands it. I can argue with them, discuss our differences, but it will always be done respectfully even though I abhor their stance. While your boss might be an idiot, the position of boss deserves respect. It's the same way I look at the president of the United States. I don't always respect the person, but I always respect the office. Some of what people say about the president (no matter who it is) is shameful and they should be embarrassed by their lack of respect. Disagree with him. Hate his actions. Despise his policies. But respect the office.

Respect is a core value. A core value that too many have abandoned. Maybe it's because they don't see what they do as being disrespectful. At least, I hope that is the case. I can't stand the thought of people knowing they are being disrespectful and being able to justify it. So I want to take some of the things I see going on and point out why I believe these things are the result of a collapse of the core value of respect.

People text and drive out of a lack of respect for themselves, their families, other people, and for life itself. If they did respect these things, they wouldn't be putting so many at risk, including themselves.

If you are 30 years old and still live at home, it's because of a lack of self-respect and a lack of respect for your parents. The same goes for parents who let their adult children live at home or support them financially. Such parents don't respect themselves and don't respect their kids enough to force them to become self-sufficient and take care of themselves.

The guy who runs the red light does it out of a lack of respect for the others who are waiting, not because he is in a hurry.

People who park in a fire zone because they can't be inconvenienced to park in the parking lot and walk all that way to the front door of the store do it because they don't respect others. They also don't respect firefighters who might be called on a moment's notice and need to use that space to save the lives of hundreds of others.

People who park in parking reserved for disable people don't respect disabled people or old people who actually need those spaces. Their convenience is more important than the fact that a disabled person might have to drive around until one of those spaces opens up or might have to park and put himself in a difficult, painful situation.

People who cut lines don't respect the people who got there earlier than they did and are already in line.

People who are lazy at work, don't show up on time, take long breaks and lunch hours don't respect their cow-orkers, the company that pays them, or their customers.

People who are late are disrespectful.

Letting your employees get by with not working is disrespectful to those who are working.

I could type pages of these examples and would love doing it. However, be completely clear about this: A lack of courtesy to others is rooted in a lack of respect and shows just how little we value others.

I was raised to always think of the impact of my actions and words on others first. My parents always asked me to reflect on how my actions made others feel and they asked me to think about whether someone else was inconvenienced in any way. I learned to live thinking about others first. That didn't make me weak or subservient but instead made me stronger. It made me think of my life as a service and about adding value to every situation instead of detracting from it. I have not always done this for sure, and I'm now very sorry about the times I did not.

RESPECT AND RACISM, SEXISM, AGEISM, WEALTHISM, AND HOMOPHOBIA

I am an older, white, straight, educated male who has money. I get told that on social media every time I post an opinion that differs from those of people who are not older, not white, not straight, not educated, and who don't have money. I guess that being what I am disqualifies me from having an opinion about issues. I get told that because I am white, I don't have the right to have an opinion on things that affect people of color. Because I am straight, my opinions on LGBT issues aren't valid. Because I am older, I have no clue about millennials. Because I am not in college, I am out of touch with what should happen on a college campus. Because I have money (now) I don't have any right to talk about the plight of the poor. You get the picture. It's interesting to me that telling me these things refutes the point they are trying to make. Telling me that my opinions don't matter because I am older, white, educated, straight or have money is racist, sexist, and homophobic. So as you read this next part, understand that attacking me because of my views on any of these issues because of who I am is exactly the problem I am addressing.

The inability to respect the differences between us all is the cause of racism, sexism, ageism, wealthism, homophobia, and all the other words and -isms associated with hate of anyone different from you. There are some people who will always hate anyone who isn't just like them, whether it's about race, sexual orientation, country of origin, money, age, or things as ridiculous as weight or color of hair. "What? Color of hair?" You've never heard a blonde joke? Or a ginger joke?

Black lives matter. Blue lives matter. White lives matter. Gay lives matter. And on and on and on. Let's be clear: all lives matter. To say anything other than that is to value one group above another. Identifying one as more important degrades and excludes the other. That is not just racist, it's wrong at a very deep level. Everyone matters. Refuse to let anyone or any group or any media coverage ever convince you of anything other than the thought that all lives matter. People demand inclusiveness to support their group's value and never stop to think about how their words do just the opposite by devaluing another group. It needs to stop.

There will always be issues between the races. And I am not just talking about blacks and whites. There is tension between all of the races at some level. It's always been that way and will always be that way. Some people just don't like anyone who looks or thinks or acts differently than they do. That is not going to change. You can't legislate it as no law is going to work to do away with racism. To think otherwise is naïve.

While we have been trying to deal with race relations for years on many levels, we continue to fail at fixing the causes of most of the problems that lead to racial problems. Education and joblessness are the core causes of our problems with race in the United States.

As far as homophobia is concerned: All of you bozos who are scared to death that letting two males who love each other or two women who love each other marry or adopt a child is going to destroy our society, wake up. You talk about the Bible and quote scripture about how wrong it is and use that to validate your hate. Well, as long as you are looking stuff up in your book, look up the part about loving each other. Interesting how so many Christians pick and choose which parts of the Bible they want to practice. And even more interesting how they use a book that teaches love to justify their hate.

I don't care who you love. Really. I know that will surprise many of my far right followers and fans. I will get hate mail about it. I will hear from many of you telling me how deeply disappointed you are in me and that you will never read my stuff or follow me again. Good. Don't. I am perfectly okay with disappointing you. I disappoint myself pretty regularly and I've learned to deal with it so you can, too; and if you can't, buh-bye! I didn't wake up today to make any of you happy, anyway, so if my opinions about gay marriage bother you . . . tough.

I do my best to live my life by my core values. One of those core values is respect. Another is being caring. Another is love. These values allow me to accept people. I don't always agree with people or the choices they make. That should be obvious. But I still accept people for who they are.

Someone being gay has no impact on me. None. It doesn't cost me any money. Their homosexuality has no impact on my heterosexuality. Them loving another person of the same sex has no impact on me at any level. It has no impact on you, either. And I don't believe it undermines the fabric of society. Besides, that fabric already is worn thin and has plenty of holes in it caused by issues that are much more important than worrying about who loves whom.

So two women (or men), who are in a loving, commit-ted relationship want to adopt a baby. They are financially stable and qualified to be parents in every way. Why are so many people against these folks having a child? We have tens of thousands of unwanted children who need homes. Why would you prefer them not to have a home rather than be loved by a couple who want them and will love them and take care of them? Do you think gay is contagious? Just what the hell are you afraid of? Get over it.

You want respect for your beliefs, your skin color, your sexual orientation, your age, your financial status, and everything else about yourself. How do you get it? Start by giving respect to others on all of those same issues.

RESPECT IS NOT JUST ABOUT RESPECTING PEOPLE

I recently discovered that many women who shop at very high-end stores buy gowns or party dresses, take them home and wear them to the party, then return them for a full refund, saying they don't like the dress. A friend who works at Neiman's tells me this happens every holiday season. The dress may have sweat stains or show other visible signs of wear, but these women have no issue with returning the dress. And unbelievably, the store takes the dress back. This is a clear lack of integrity and respect on the part of the customer. If you are reading this and laughing because you do this, you should be ashamed of yourself. In essence, you stole the dress so you could wear it to the party. You didn't even rent it as the store didn't make any money from the dress. The store lost money because all they got back was a used dress that can't be sold again. How would you feel about buying a dress you thought was new but in reality had been worn by someone else and returned? This also speaks to the core values of the stores that allow this insanity. Evidently, they value keeping a customer who is dishonest and lacks integrity more than they do the dress. Their argument is that the customer will spend enough money throughout the year to more than cover the cost of the dress. Not the point.

I was in a very nice restaurant where a person at the table next to me ordered a lobster. He then ate half of the lobster before he said that it was overcooked and wanted another one. They brought another, and, again he ate half of it and declared it tough and asked for another that he was finally satisfied with and ate to completion. So, he got three full lobsters for the price of one. When the guy left, I asked the waiter about it. He said that the guy does it every time and they know he is just getting three lobsters for the price of one but that he spends enough money there to cover it. Okay, I understand profitability quite well, but at some point, customer abuse becomes your company's core value if you knowingly allow your customers to make a fool of you like this. At some point, you have to respect yourself and your business enough to tell this customer that you no longer need, want, or will accept his business.

Some of you are probably saying, "Larry, aren't you going a little far with these examples? Is it that big of a deal?" Yes, it's a big deal. The collapse of core values is a slippery slope. Start to compromise on the little things and the big things aren't far away.

Religion, traditions, and holidays all deserve respect even if you don't practice the same ones. Me saying "Merry Christmas" doesn't hurt you in any way, so shut up about it. Me celebrating Christmas doesn't keep you from celebrating your religious holiday, so respect my celebration and go celebrate yours. I promise I will respect you when you do.

Respect is also about knowing that you need to practice more self-respect. If you tolerate being mistreated by others through their words or their actions, you don't respect yourself. If you allow companies to give you bad service and you continue to accept it, you don't respect yourself or your money. You must have enough self-respect to speak up on your own behalf and make it known to the offender and stop doing business with such an entity.

To allow yourself to be disrespected is to give up your personal power. I don't give my personal power away. It's not up for grabs to anyone. No one can take it from me. That's because I have self-respect. When I tell people this, they say, "Well, you're lucky." No luck has been involved in my development of this trait. I was taught this from birth. My folks instilled this in me and reinforced it daily. It was a core value their parents taught them and they, in turn, taught it to me.

Self-respect can be taken too far. Sometimes, concern with being respected slides into becoming overly sensitive. I am about to address the issue of being overly sensitive, but it is important to note here that much of that is about an overblown sense of self-respect, which turns out to be disrespect of others.

One of the biggest issues with having a lack of respect is that it often results in a lack of civility.

Civility is sadly lacking in our society. Civility is politeness in speech and behavior, and it creates safety for a diversity of opinions and dialogue.

Uncivil people believe that disagreeing with another's opinion makes it okay to slander, denigrate, or be rude to that person. Bad behavior is justified because the uncivil person is unhappy with what another says or does. It demonstrates a fundamental disrespect not only for the other party but for society as a whole, effectively polluting it with unnecessary vitriol.

Ultimately, a lack of civility rooted in a lack of respect stifles freedom of speech. More on that to come.

PEOPLE ARE OFFENDED BY DAMN NEAR EVERYTHING!

Welcome to the Butthurt States of America

Some of you are already offended simply because I just used the word butthurt. What you should be more offended by is that it has become so real and so common in our society that it has recently been added to the Oxford Dictionary.

Here is the definition from the dictionary: "Overly or unjustifiably offended or resentful."

Did reading that definition bring some things to mind? How about some people? I am sure you can think of lots of folks in your life who are walking around looking for something to be offended about. I know I can. I would love to just list their names right here and publish them for the whole world to see.

Since some folks are so desperately looking for something to be offended about, I have made it my goal not to disappoint them by giving them plenty to work with.

Let's be clear about what being butthurt really is. It is a desperate attempt for people to bring attention to themselves. It is the practice of weak people who are eager to play the victim. Yes, there really are people who want to play the victim. Being a victim on purpose is the ultimate power play. It allows the poor souls to control the situation and the emotions and reactions of others. Please note that the definition says "overly" and "unjustifiably." There are reasons to be offended. But being butthurt has nothing to do with those reasons. Butthurt is being *overly* offended and *unjustifiably* offended.

Being a butthurt victim allows these miserable people to bring attention to their real or fantasized issues so others will react. And these folks don't really care what the reaction is. When a child wants attention, she will act out in order to get attention. Sometimes that attention is positive and sometimes it is negative. The person receiving the attention doesn't really care; she just wants attention. That is the core issue for the butthurt: they want attention. When confronted with this notion, they will get indignant and say that it is the cause or the injustice they are fighting for. No, it's attention they are fighting for.

Before you get all butthurt and offended, ask yourself why it bothers you so much.

Maybe the problem is you, not it.

Only the weak are constantly offended by things that have nothing to do with them.

This phenomenon of butthurtedness is a relatively new thing. We haven't always been bothered so much by things. Especially, by words. Stupid people would say stupid things to you and you shrugged it off. You didn't cry about it. You didn't run to the teacher or to the school administration. You didn't even run to mama and daddy. You got over it. Or you did something about it. You got mad and addressed it. You stood up for yourself. Where did that go?

I made a decision to do whatever it took to become successful when I was 13 years old when another eighth-grade kid made fun of me for being so poor that I only had one pair of jeans. Those words hurt my feelings. But I didn't cry about it and I didn't tell on him. Instead, I made a decision. Those words caused me to become determined to never be humiliated for being poor again. The first thing I did was go out and get a really crappy job to buy myself a new pair of jeans. And I've been working ever since. So I thank God that kid said those words to me. Today, that kid would be called a bully. Back then, he was just a kid who said something insensitive to another kid. He didn't need to be reprimanded or sent home for being a bully. The newspapers didn't need to know about it. My parents didn't need to know about it. No one needed to read about it on Facebook. It was an incident that lasted five seconds. But those five seconds changed my life. If I had been born 50 years later, I might have found myself running to a safe zone where no one could say anything that could hurt my feelings. I would be living in a society where you are not allowed to use words that humiliate or belittle.

I understand that words can hurt. And I hate what some people say to others regarding their race or sexual orientation and any number of other things. However, no one can ever or should ever be protected from words, even when the words hurt. Instead, we should use those words to instigate an exchange of ideas, open discussion, and create understanding. You can't legislate kindness. You can't legislate common sense. It must be taught.

No one can be or should be protected from words, even when those words are hurtful.

Stupid people say stupid things. People are idiots, they've always been idiots, and they are always going to be idiots. Everyone? No, luckily not everyone is an idiot. But there will be enough of them out there to make you crazy if you let them. The key is not to let them.

People are going to say stupid things to you. You can whine and cry and look for your safe place or you can just understand that some people are going to say stupid things. You will go to school with these people, work with these people, go to church with these people, and, sometimes, these people will be a part of your own family.

People will be racist. People will be misogynistic. People will be homophobic. People are going to hate you for who you are, what you stand for, the color of your skin, your sexual orientation, the way you part your hair, the fact you don't have any hair, because you have freckles, are a Republican, are a Democrat, don't vote, do vote, or because you are a Christian, a Jew, a Muslim, a Hindu, an atheist, or agnostic. Pick something. In fact, pick anything, and people are going to hate you for it. Here's an idea for you: Let that be *their* problem, not yours. The instant you start to feel like you are being picked on or victimized, you have given someone else power over your life. Just find satisfaction that these people are idiots and you aren't.

Does that mean what they say and do doesn't hurt? Not at all. The stupidity of others can hurt a lot.

Does it mean you shouldn't speak up against it? No, it doesn't mean that, either. We should all speak up for ourselves and our beliefs.

Does it mean they are going to stop being that way? That's not happening. People have always been idiots and always will be.

You can let it ruin your day or you can understand it and move on. Sadly, most folks can't do this, and too many let it ruin not only their day but their lives.

I fully support everyone's right to say what they want. I even support an idiot's right to say idiotic things. The Constitution protects that right as well. There are many of us who would fight for every other American's right to say whatever they want to say. In fact, many have fought and died for that right and others. Sadly, there are some who would only fight for the right to say whatever they want to say and not what you or I want to say.

Freedom of speech is a two-way street. You get to say what you want to say and I get to say what I want to say. We both get to speak, whether the other one likes it or not. Even if it hurts your feelings. Even if it hurts my feelings. Even if it's stupid. That's the way free speech works. Too many do not believe in freedom *of* speech but instead freedom *from* speech they don't want to hear.

Here is what people need to remember: While we all have the right to say pretty much whatever we want, even stupid things, even hurtful things, we all also have the right not to be bothered by speech. In fact, we have more than a right; I believe we have an obligation. We are obligated for our own sanity and safety to not be bothered by every hurtful or stupid thing we hear.

They are *words*! It's not a baseball bat you are being hit with. There is no physical damage. You aren't going to die from them. "But Larry! There is emotional and psychological damage!" Not if you refuse to allow the words to hurt you. Every person has the power to refuse to allow themselves to be hurt by the words of others. Is it hard? Sometimes. Does it take practice? Sometimes. But it is based on a psyche of self-respect and self-worth.

Parents need to teach that idea to their kids. School systems need to reinforce it instead of creating safe zones so it can't and won't happen (more on that to come), and society needs to stop promoting this whole butthurt agenda.

In other words, we all need to put on our big-boy pants; stop being so thin-skinned; stop being whining, narcissistic crybabies and grow the hell up.

Political correctness is what started us down this slippery slope into becoming the butthurt wimps we have become. Know how I know that? I know that some of you right now are butthurt because in that sentence I just wrote, you are upset that I said "big-boy pants" and that isn't inclusive for all the women out there. I'm right and you know it. We have become oversensitized to even simple phrases like that one.

I said in my book *Grow a Pair* that political correctness is the most castrating thing that has happened to our society.

Our oversensitivity to everything has pushed us into an unhealthy place. It has separated us, not unified us. Political correctness, in most cases, creates a problem where none previously existed. And it has gone off the rails.

There is a movement now that groups not be allowed to applaud at conferences because applause triggers anxiety. They suggest the use of jazz hands instead of applause. Go ahead and laugh, it's appropriate.

People want trigger warnings before they hear certain words because those words upset them. One college student told me she was afraid of tornados and she needed a trigger warning if that word was to be used around her. Must be hard to watch a weather report. Hope she decides not to live in Oklahoma! Words like alcohol, blood, insects, rape, even animals in wigs are considered triggers in some situations. I don't get it (well, maybe I get animals in wigs). If words can trigger you, I suggest you stay off the Internet, turn off your television, never read a book or have a conversation, and crawl back into your baby bed with your blankie and cover up your head. In fact, please do that as I don't want to know you even exist.

The Department of Justice recently announced that the agency will no longer call people "felons" or "convicts" after they are released from prison because it is too hard on them emotionally. Poor babies. Maybe prison hurt their feelings too. Should we have let them slide on their time as well?

But let's get to the most offensive culprit of being offended: colleges and college professors. College professors do more to enable butthurtedness than any other group of people in society.

A professor at North Carolina State University decided to dock her students' grades for using what she considered to be sexist language in class assignments. In her syllabus, she wrote these words: "You may *not* use 'he' or 'him,' or 'man' to refer to both men and women." The professor told students they can replace "mankind" with "humans" or "humankind," and should write "she or he" instead of just "he."

Here's another one from Tennessee: "Educators in the Volunteer State are very concerned that students might be offended by the usage of traditional pronouns like she, he, him and her, according to a document (www.utk.edu/diversity/) from the University of Tennessee–Knoxville's Office of Diversity and Inclusion."

Donna Braquet, the director of the university's Pride Center, suggested using a variety of gender-neutral pronouns instead of traditional pronouns. "There are dozens of gender-neutral pronouns," she declared. (Here are some of the new gender-neutral pronouns she's talking about: ze, hir, xe, xem, and xyr). "These may sound a little funny at first, but only because they are new," Braquet explained. "The 'she' and 'he' pronouns would sound strange, too, if we had been taught 'ze' when growing up."

Insanity? You think? Watering down our language in an effort to protect a bunch of eager-to-be-butthurt kids who weren't taught that she, he, him, and her are *not* offensive words. Being butthurt by them, however, is extremely offensive to ze. I mean me.

Professors like this are not making this county better. They are not creating stronger, more responsible, pro-ductive citizens. They are adding to the already growing number of hypersensitive butthurt people looking to be taken care of by a benevolent society and government.

The University of Kansas allows people on campus to choose their own gender by wearing a pin with their chosen gender on it. "Because gender is, itself, fluid and up to the individual, each person has the right to identify their own pronouns, and we encourage you to ask before assuming someone's gender," a sign in the library above the available buttons reads.

I know the subject of gender is a sensitive issue to discuss right now in the United States. And I am sensitive to people who are attempting to come to grips with who they are and need support for their struggle and their decision. But it has simply become too complicated for me. Facebook now allows 51 gender identities to choose from. You can now label yourself as gender nonconforming, agender, bigender, transgender, pangender, gender variant, gender diverse, and even genderless. You can even decide to be other or neither. In my way of thinking, you can choose neither as a label but can't actually be neither: you are something whether you choose it or not. You can even be something called "two-spirit."

This is the castration of common sense. There is a huge segment of society, seemingly led by educated college professors, that are doing their dead level best to neuter society to the point where we no longer have men and women but one huge genderless mass. This genderless society will belittle men and women who unashamedly are secure in their masculinity and femininity. Those of us with a pair (not between our legs but between our ears) must not allow this to happen!

Now, back to university professors: I prefer this example from Mike Adams, criminology professor at the University of North Carolina, Wilmington. This is an excerpt from his introduction to class.

> Welcome back to class, students! I am Mike Adams, your criminology professor here at UNC-Wilmington. Before we get started with the course I need to address an issue that is causing problems here at UNCW and in higher education all across the country. I am talking about the growing minority of students who believe they have a right to be free from being offended. If we don't reverse this dangerous trend in our society there will soon be a majority of young people who will need to walk around in plastic bubble suits to protect them in the event that they come into contact with a dissenting viewpoint. That mentality is unworthy of an American. It's hardly worthy of a Frenchman. Let's get something straight right now. You have no right to be unoffended. You have a right to be offended with regularity. It is the price you pay for living in a free society. If you don't understand that, you are confused and dangerously so.

This is the slippery slope I mentioned earlier. And part of sliding down that slope dumps us into the safe zone area.

I know that the original intent of safe zones was to create places where LGBT students could go to be physically safe from harm. That's fine, as no one should be physically attacked for being who they are. But like so many things, the original intent got corrupted, hijacked, and bastardized, and these safe zones grew into places where you can run so as to not have your feelings hurt.

How bad is it? Well, bad enough that students at California State University, Los Angeles needed a safe space to deal with the pain they were caused because conservative commentator Ben Shapiro spoke on their campus. But here's the amazing part: the speech happened two months earlier and wasn't attended by the people who needed the safe space to get over the emotional and psychological trauma. How many ways can we say crybaby? Parents of those kids, are you proud of your precious little snowflakes? Are you glad you are spending your money to send them to a place that would tolerate this nonsense? Are you glad you coddled your brats and made them a pain in the ass for the rest of us?

Or how about Emory University in Atlanta where Vote Trump appeared on college sidewalks? One student told the campus paper, "I'm supposed to feel comfortable and safe here. But this man is being supported by students on our campus and our administration shows that they, by their silence, support it as well. I don't deserve to feel afraid at my school." The college bowed to this stupidity and offered counseling to the offended students. What did that cost us all?

When a person's name can cause you trauma, you are a wuss. You have no reason to be on a college campus. You are still a two-year-old child scared of the boogeyman. And if you are a college student and the name of a candidate for president of the United States of America throws you into a panic to the point you need counseling, you are not going to be able to survive in the real world. Go home to mama and please, never apply for a job. No company needs you or wants you.

Cleveland College even set up safe zones and counseling because the Republican National Convention was held in its city. Holy crap, this stuff drives me *nuts*! And to make it worse, these colleges receive federal funding. Your tax dollars at work!

LUCKILY SOME PEOPLE ARE SPEAKING UP AGAINST THIS STUPIDITY

Michael Bloomberg, billionaire and former mayor of New York City, said this in his commencement address at the University of Michigan:

> The most useful knowledge that you leave here with today is how to study, cooperate, listen carefully, think critically, and resolve conflicts through reason. Those are the most important skills in the working world, and it's why colleges have always exposed students to challenging and uncomfortable ideas.
>
> The fact that some university boards and administrations now bow to pressure and shield students from these ideas through "safe spaces," "code words," and "trigger warnings" is, in my view, a terrible mistake.
>
> The whole purpose of college is to learn how to deal with difficult situations—not run away from them. A microaggression is exactly that: micro. And one of the most dangerous places on a college campus is a safe space, because it creates a false impression that we can insulate ourselves from those who hold different views.

We can't do this, and we shouldn't try—not in politics or in the workplace. In the global economy, and in a democratic society, an open mind is the most valuable asset you can possess.

There are many areas where I disagree with Mr. Bloomberg. However, in this case, he is 100 percent correct. Sadly, the students booed him for these words.

I wish Mr. Bloomberg's message could be heard by the students of Oberlin College who issued what they called "not a polite request, but a concrete and unmalleable demand to create special, segregated, black-only safe spaces across campus." Guess they are unaware that segregation ended. I think Martin Luther King Jr. is probably rolling over in his grave over this.

These examples are just a few of the many, many sad ones that are out there. They are proof of what has happened to our educational system because we have let our core values disintegrate. It's proof that we are failing our country by failing our kids.

One final example is the story of Yale University students who eagerly signed a petition to repeal the First Amendment. Some, of course, had to have it read to them first, but then were all for signing the petition to abolish free speech. One student told the person with the petition how "awesome" it was he was out there doing this. Amazing that these Ivy League students didn't understand that one element of the First Amendment is the right to petition, which they were signing a petition to abolish.

To be intentionally offensive is wrong.
To be intentionally offended is ridiculous.

PEOPLE ALLOW TECHNOLOGY TO RULE THEIR LIVES

Teens spend nine hours per day on average on a device. That's more time than they spend sleeping or with their teachers or parents. And that doesn't include any time spent on a device at school doing schoolwork. But it's not just teens; kids between the ages of 8 and 12 spend about six hours.

Ninety-one percent of people between the ages of 15 and 34 use Facebook.

A recent Pew Research survey of adults in the United States found that 71 percent use Facebook at least occasionally, and 45 percent of Facebook users check the site several times a day.

I am convinced that kids who grow up with some sort of device in their hands all of the time end up with some sort of communications disorder. Can I prove it? Nope, but it sure seems to me that people don't have the ability to look you in the eye and have a basic conversation like they did before texting.

I'm sick of seeing families out for dinner at a restaurant where every member of the family has their nose stuck in a screen. It is destroying our ability to communicate with each other and it is destroying our families.

Seeing a kid with a cell phone or an iPad in her hand makes me sad. I would much rather see a coloring book or—wait—a *real* book.

And while technology is killing our ability to socialize and communicate, in too many cases, it's literally killing us.

Some of you are going to kill the rest of us simply because you believe your text is more important than your life. Put your damn phone down before you kill yourself and someone else.

Let's look at some scary statistics about texting and driving:

- The National Safety Council reported that cell phone use while driving leads to 1.6 million crashes each year.
- There are nearly 330,000 injuries each year from accidents caused by texting while driving.
- Texting while driving causes 25% of all car accidents in the United States.
- Texting while driving leads to the death of 11 teens every day.
- Half of all teenagers admit to texting and driving.

CHAPTER THREE

WHAT'S WRONG WITH BUSINESS

What's wrong with business? Plenty, I can assure you. Let's start with the basics.

WHY DO BUSINESSES EXIST?

People get so confused about this one. Too many believe that the business exists to take care of them: to make sure they have a nice, comfortable place to go to pass their time and visit with friends and play on the Internet and to get paid however much it takes to support their chosen lifestyle. Then you have those who believe business exists as a place of toil and heartache where the mean old bosses expect them to actually break a sweat to support their greed. A place where they are committed to giving as little as possible—just enough to keep from getting fired—and they are convinced that they are the targets of billionaire CEOs who stand on the necks of the little guy who makes it all possible. Then there is that group who honestly don't care. They are so apathetic that they make no connection with their own effort and what is actually being done at the business that pays them. As a customer, you can always spot these folks, can't you? Phones stuck to their ears, and upon seeing a customer they roll their eyes and begrudgingly tell their friends, "I have to go, some asshole wants something." Well, to these folks and all the other categories of employees out there, here is a revelation for you: businesses exist to make money. Yep, that's it. Their sole goal is profitability. Sounds completely soulless doesn't it? But for those of you thinking that, here is another revelation you might consider: businesses that are profitable understand they get that way by filling a need and serving their customer well. Yeah, they make money for doing so and that is their purpose, but they understand how they make money, too.

So if you think the business you work for (or pretend to work for) is there to take care of you, or to make you happy, or to protect you from getting your feelings hurt, you need a reality check. It is there to make money. Be glad it does, because that money pays your salary and insurance. You need to contribute to the company's profitability by serving their customers well. Do that and you'll have a very successful career. If you don't, every boss you work for will see you for what you are: a pain-in-the-ass employee. You will be passed over for every promotion that comes along simply because you are a burden and an expense rather than an asset.

Let's look more at what is wrong with business and people's unrealistic expectations of what business is about and what they should expect from employment.

Companies do not pay you to help you achieve your
dreams. Achieving your dreams is up to you. They pay
you so you can help them achieve their dreams. Understand that and honor the deal you made when you took
the job.

Loving What You Do

There is an old quote people love to use to support the idea
that you should love what you do. "If you love what you do,
you will never work a day in your life."

The quote has been attributed to lots of people, so I
can't pin this stupidity on any one person. Too bad, as I
would love to.

People who use this line are people who have probably
never really worked a day in their life. Even if that work is
something they love to do. I don't care how much you love
something, eventually it becomes work!

I have told the story many times from the stage that I
hate what I do for a living. The audience gasps in some
cases. I love that part! I go on to explain that they think that
standing on stages giving my speech is what I do for a
living. No. I do that about 75 hours a year. I travel about
150 days a year to do that 75 hours of speaking. I love the
75 hours of speaking and hate nearly every minute of the
150 days of travel. The key is that I love the 75 hours of
speaking enough to put up with the 150 days of travel.

And it doesn't matter what you do or how much you
love it. You can love fishing but if you did it for a living,
eventually it would become work.

You can love baking cookies. At home. In your kitchen. For your kids. You say to yourself, "If I could just bake cookies for a living, I would *love* it! I would never complain. Nothing could possibly ever be better than baking cookies for a living." Then you find yourself in a commercial kitchen, with several ovens, dozens of employees, thousands of demanding customers, government regulation, taxes, and more, and your passion and your love of baking has become a job and there are many parts that you flat out hate.

If you are set on loving something about your business, try this: love what you do enough to become amazing at it. There is nothing more rewarding than being amazing at what you do. It will make you more valuable to your employer and your customers and it's the quickest way to give yourself a raise.

It's amazing how being good at something makes you like doing it more. Before you decide you don't like doing something, become excellent at it.

THE BIGGEST CHALLENGE FACING BUSINESS

I see the biggest challenge as an entitled, unskilled workforce. I've already been crystal clear about my belief that too many children are overprotected, sheltered from disappointment, not allowed to experience failure, and believe they are owed a living.

Just as alarming is the new Princeton study that says millennials in the United States are the least skilled in the world. They ranked last in literacy and basic math skills, can't follow directions, and can't use technology well enough to use it on a job. A Bentley University study found that 60 percent of millennials are not considering a career in business and 48 percent say they have not been encouraged to do so. Yet, in the next 5 to 10 years millennials will make up the majority of the workforce.

We used to say that education was about the 3 Rs: Reading, wRiting, and aRithmetic. Add two more: Responsibility and Respect. Those five are our issues and will be our downfall.

Scared yet? You should be. If we are to save U.S. businesses from going outside of our country to hire a qualified workforce, parents must do their jobs and force school systems to do theirs.

To solve this impending crisis, we are going to have to do the following things.

Parental Responsibility

- Parents are going to have to teach their children the core value of self-sufficiency.
- Parents are going to have to stop being enablers of their children. Parents need to teach the skills necessary for success: work ethic; communications; and respect for authority, coworkers, and customers.
- Parents are going to have to force more accountability on school systems to teach basic skills.
- Parents are going to need to guide their children toward an education in marketable skills.

School Systems

- School systems must make sure that kids can read, write, do basic math, and follow directions.
- Schools also need to teach computer skills that are useful in the business world.
- Schools are going to have to refuse to pass kids who can't do the necessary work.

Business Training

- Businesses must grasp the concept that the cost of an untrained workforce is more expensive than the training.
- Businesses must be prepared to educate the new workforce since school systems and parents haven't and probably won't do their jobs.
- Businesses are going to need to budget both time and money to teach the skills they need their employees to have.

In order to turn things around in business, both bosses and employees are going to have to change a lot of what they are doing. Here are a couple of lists that every boss and employee needs to remember.

Employers Need to Remember

- If you have lousy employees, it's because you are a lousy employer. Your employees will be no better than you are. Fix yourself first. Your employees only reflect back to you who you really are as an employer and company.

- Your job is to make your company the best place for a customer to do business with. That means you must hire the best people, give them the best training, be the best example for them to emulate, and drive the concept of "value" home with every person who works there.
- Stand up for what is right. Don't even think about whether it is the easiest thing, the cheapest thing, or the fastest thing. The right thing is sometimes the hardest, the most expensive, and the slowest thing you can do. Do the right thing regardless.
- Your employees can't read your mind. Don't expect them to know what you want until you tell them and teach them.
- Hire slow. Fire fast. Most employers have this one backward.
- If you put up with it, you are endorsing it. Do you endorse rudeness, lousy service, being late, stealing, being lazy or disrespectful? No? Then why do you put up with it?

Employees Need to Remember

- You are paid to work—not to make personal calls, do your social media, or any other personal activity. Employees should stop and ask themselves, "Is this what I was hired to do and am being paid to do?" If not, you are stealing from your employer and should stop.
- You are an expense. If the cost to employ you exceeds your value, then there is no reason for the company to employ you. Always be adding to your value.

- No one likes a whiner, complainer, gossip, or troublemaker, but everyone loves a person who will do what it takes to get the job done, is willing to be of service to anyone, and can be counted on.
- Businesses don't exist to make employees happy. They want their employees to be happy, but that is not the reason they are in business. They are in business to be profitable. They do that by having products and services their customers want and by serving those customers well. It's a simple equation. Employees need to understand it and contribute to the profitability of the company in order to have job security.

Yep, I'm a hard-ass.

EMPLOYEES MUST CONSTANTLY ADD VALUE

What Are You Worth?

You typically earn what you are worth. Now, I can tell you from experience that this idea bothers nearly everybody. People love to think they are worth more than they are. And I am not talking about worth as a human being. I am talking about worth as a member of the workforce.

The guy who taught me the most, back when I first started on my own journey of personal development, was Jim Rohn. Rohn said, "People who earn $5 an hour provide $5 worth of service and it takes them an hour to do it. People who earn $5,000 an hour provide $5,000 worth of service and it takes them an hour to do it. The

difference is not the hour, the difference is in the service."
There is a profound lesson there for everyone. When you
look at your paycheck, be clear that is the amount of
service you provide and not a reflection of the number of
hours you work. It is a representation of your value in the
marketplace. It doesn't take much to say, "You want fries
with that?" That's why it isn't worth much. That's why
those jobs are rapidly being replaced with machines. You
can argue this point all you want and it won't change the
truth: you are worth what you are paid.

The key is to be worth more than you are paid, so
eventually you can be paid more. Constantly increase your
value to your employer, your customers, and to the
marketplace in general.

Be worth more than you are paid so eventually you can
be paid more.

Think of it this way: If you weren't there, how much
would you be missed? Place a number in it. That's how
much you are worth to your company. If they can just as
easily do the job without you then you aren't worth much.
If they can find someone else to take up your slack then
you aren't worth much. The more valuable you are, the
more you will be missed. That is how much you are worth.

Again, don't overestimate your worth like most people
do. Be honest with yourself. Regardless of how valuable
you think what you do is, chances are that it can be done
just as well, or maybe better, by someone else and for less
money.

The solution is to add more value every day. Figure
out how to take on a little more responsibility. Be willing

to go the extra mile. Don't constantly focus on doing just enough to get by. That is a contradiction to the core value of adding value.

There are no secrets to success.
Solve a problem.
Add value.
Be worth more than you cost.
Outwork everyone.
Repeat this process daily.

FIDUCIARY RESPONSIBILITY

When I show up to do a speech, it's because I have been paid to be there. I am not doing it because I love doing it. I am not doing it to change the world. I am not passionate about it. It's my business to give speeches. Because it's my business to give speeches, I work hard at giving the best speech I can possibly give. It comes from a commitment to excellence, which is one of my values. But it also comes from my understanding that giving the best speech I can possibly give is what my client hired me to do. It's what they paid for. It's what they expect.

There is a fiduciary responsibility for me to deliver the best possible product and service I possibly can because we have an agreement based on money exchanging hands. There is nothing emotional about it. They don't care whether I like them or feel good that day or whether I am in the mood. We are exchanging money, so I respect the transaction and the money they are paying me; I do my best no matter what.

Too many transactions between customer and business are based on conditions. How is everyone feeling at the time of the exchange: Are we all happy? In a good mood? Enjoying ourselves? Feeling okay? Let's get clear: No one cares about any of those things when they are paying money for you to perform. Customers want you to deliver the product and the service in the best possible way with the least possible complications, because that's what they are paying for. It's not an emotional exchange. It's a deal based on the exchange of money.

Respect the exchange of funds enough to realize that and do your best in every way no matter what!

Unions Are Ruining Business

People complain about prices being so high—want to know why they are? Unions. Companies can no longer afford unions' inflated demands, so the only way to pay their employees what unions negotiate is to raise prices. If they keep raising prices, eventually customers won't put up with it, and the company goes out of business. Or the government bails it out and that costs us all.

Want to know why more jobs are going overseas? Unions again. Consumers want low prices. You can't have low prices when something is made in the United States, because Americans cost so much to employ! Why do they cost so much to employ? Unions!

There is an old saying, "Don't bite the hand that feeds you." Unions have not only bitten the hand, they went ahead and gnawed off the whole arm. They went from being organizations that kept employees safe and treated fairly to vampires that are bankrupting our businesses as well as our governments. Unions have sucked the life out of budgets by demanding so much that businesses can no longer afford to pay their current employees, and governments cannot keep the doors open because they are paying for the bloated pensions of past employees.

And speaking of government unions, also known as public employee unions, I say BS. Total BS. Government employees work for the taxpayer. We pay their salaries. Federal employees are already paid 78 percent more in total compensation than private sector workers. And then they believe they have the right to demand more and to strike when they don't get it? No. Government employees work for all of us and their job is to keep the government open.

The same applies to teachers. I know they aren't paid enough. Good teachers are worth their weight in gold. However, they are paid with taxpayer money to teach our children. They can claim they need more money (and they do), but striking to get it and putting families in a bind scrambling for childcare is not the way to get it or to win community support. Holding someone hostage doesn't create a winning situation—it creates resentment. By the way, teachers knew what the salary was before they took the job, so to take the job and then complain about it because you don't like the pay is absurd.

CHAPTER FOUR

WHAT'S WRONG WITH EDUCATION

We don't value education enough in our society. Maybe it is because we fail to see that education is the solution to so many of our problems.

A better-educated society is a more employable society. People with jobs are less likely to turn to crime—less likely to turn to drugs, prostitution, robbery, assault, and more. They are more likely to stay home and take care of their families. They have money to spend, which helps the economy. They are also less dependent on the government to take care of them.

Sadly, most folks have never stepped back and looked at the big picture and end up focusing on the wrong solutions to many of our problems. Want to fight drugs, racism, teen pregnancy, government dependence? Get more kids in school and keep them there.

As a country, we are failing at this as the following statistics show.

- Every 26 seconds, a high school student drops out of school—7,000 students per day.
- Twenty-five percent of high school freshmen fail to graduate on time.

- The United States now ranks 22nd out of 27 developed countries in graduation rates.
- The average income of a high school dropout is about $20,000 per year while a high school graduate earns over $36,000 per year.

These stats alone should be all you need to know that we have a crisis of education in our country.

But the problem is not confined to our high school dropout statistics. Education as a core value means we have to look past just these numbers.

College is the next issue. I am not a fan of free college. I am not supportive of the government loaning money to students. Anytime the government gets involved in financing anything at any level, the price goes up. I firmly believe that one of the reasons college costs so much is because government pays for tuition for so many and colleges know that they can charge whatever they want because the government is paying for it. Therefore, I am a fan of a more affordable college experience. I believe that work-study programs make sense. I still fully support military service and the GI Bill. I like an exchange of community service for financial aid. I like what some Texas colleges are doing by allowing students with military, work, and life experience to test out of many of their college courses. I think there are many alternative avenues to the government loaning money to students. It's not good for education, it's not good for the student, and it's not good for the government. The government needs out of the loaning money business.

Here is my biggest issue with a college education: It's just not the solution it once was. Don't expect your kid to go to college and graduate on Tuesday and have a high-paying job on Wednesday. It doesn't work that way anymore. Yeah, it does for some, so don't start telling me about your genius nephew who had 14 job offers waiting for him. That's not the norm. For many kids, a college degree is an expensive piece of paper that they will spend years paying for and will have little to do with the job they end up taking—especially when you have so many students graduating with no marketable skills. Parents, you must guide your children to study subjects that have a financially viable future.

The chances are not good that your children will become self-sufficient and be able to support themselves if you allow them to take college courses in things like Lady Gaga and the Sociology of Fame, What If Harry Potter Is Real, Philosophy and Star Trek, Invented Lan guages: Klingon and Beyond, Zombies in Popular Media, and The Textual Appeal of Tupac Shakur. Yes, these are real college courses. I could name another hundred that are just as stupid. We don't need more courses in under-water basket weaving. We need more math and science. We need basic literacy courses. We need courses on financial literacy. We need courses that actually prepare kids for the marketplace.

And when I said, "if you allow your children" I mean exactly what I said. You are the adult, you are probably paying, and you should know better and care enough not to allow this to happen.

In fact, maybe you should take a good hard look at college for your children. I can guarantee you that most plumbers make more money than most philosophy majors. Why? Toilets aren't going away and everyone's toilet eventually breaks.

And don't give me the argument of following your bliss. For too many kids today, following their bliss means sitting in their bedrooms at the age of 25, eating Mama's cooking, and playing video games while robbing their parents of their retirement. Bliss be damned, get a damn job!

And for too many, attending college is not much more than an excuse to delay entering the workforce just so they can do what I just described.

We have an abundance of jobs in this country that do not require a college degree. There are hundreds of thousands of blue-collar jobs that need to be filled right now. The problem is that too many view those jobs as demeaning. The "too many" I am referring to are parents who dreamed of "better" for their kids. I never dreamed of better for my kids. I only dreamed of them being employed, independent, good people who had a strong work ethic, integrity, were honest, and men of high moral fiber. Fortunately, I ended up with that. But I never saw a college degree as the only way for them to achieve that. We need to get over our elitist attitudes about blue-collar jobs and stop looking down our noses at the many honorable, high-paying jobs that require you to break a sweat and know how to use a tool. Our society would fold like a cheap suit if these jobs failed to exist. That's why there is great job security in providing these services.

I believe we need to put shop classes back in public schools. I believe that we need financial literacy classes in public schools. I even believe home economics should be brought back into the curriculum. There is nothing sexist or wrong about teaching both boys and girls the basics about nutrition, basic cooking skills, hygiene, home finance, and more.

I also believe we need to put more emphasis on vocational technical schools. We need to hold this type of education in higher esteem and encourage the many, many kids who just aren't cut out for college to enter these schools instead of traditional four-year colleges. At least kids who graduate from technical schools almost always have a good job.

I am also a big believer in the military as an option for many kids. The very best thing that happened to my son was going into the military. College was not the right choice for him. The Army was. He was a pretty good kid when he went in but he came out a fine young man. Those eight years were the best investment in his future he could possibly have made.

PARENTAL INVOLVEMENT

While parents need to flex their muscles when it comes to guiding their children about what direction to take as they enter college or determining whether college is right for them at all, there is a time when parents need to butt out.

When I was a kid and got in trouble, my parents didn't go to the teacher to complain. They let the teacher discipline me and then they disciplined me. They didn't second-guess the teacher. They trusted the teacher, as the adult, to judge if I was wrong. They never blamed the teacher when I got in trouble, either. My, how things have changed!

Now when a kid gets in trouble and the parent is notified, the kid is immediately the victim. The parent calls the 6 o'clock news team and the television van rolls up to find some wailing mama talking about how her precious snowflake has been mistreated. Never mind that the precious snowflake cussed out and slugged a teacher. Their *baby* has been maligned! Holy crap people! Chances are very high that your baby was wrong and got less than he deserved, anyway.

Now, does that mean that all teachers and schools make good decisions and can't be wrong in these situations? I'm not saying that at all. But most of the time, the teacher is right and your kid is wrong. And my response is almost always going to be, "you do the crime, you do the time." Let your kid be punished.

By the way, I have a keen sense of being able to predict responses to my writing. This last statement will cause many of you to write bad reviews of this book and write me letters. Do what you want, make yourself happy. You won't be able to change my mind, so have at it.

If you want to become involved in your kid's life at school, go to PTA meetings. Go to parent/teacher conferences. Volunteer to help out in the classroom. Talk to your kid about school, and their friends, and the work they are doing.

FAILURE *IS* AN OPTION

When I was in school we had kids that were two or three years older than the rest of us in our class. Why? They were failed and held back until they could do the work and pass the requisite tests. What was the downside to that action? None that I can see except they were no fun to play dodgeball against. Some of them were damn near grown men with beards! Did holding them back hurt their feel-ings? Don't know and don't care. School was about teaching information and you stayed where you were until you learned the information. Now we have to save every child's fragile little psyche from experiencing failure of any type for fear of permanent damage. Ridiculous. Passing kids who can't do the work isn't fair to the kids who can do the work. And it's also not fair to the kid who couldn't do the work but was passed anyway. Teaching our kids they can get by with inferior performance has led to one of the huge problems afflicting many people today. It's what leads to entitlement mentality. It's what makes folks who mumble, "You want fries with that?" believe that that level of skill is worth $15 an hour.

Some of our school systems don't want our kids to experience the pain of failing. File this next piece in the "You aren't going to believe this shit" category. School officials at Yeshiva Ketana of Long Island sent the follow-ing letter to parents along with their child's grades:

> Since our goal is to share accurate information with the parents, and not to discourage or hurt a student, great discretion must be used before allowing your child to review his report card. Certainly, report cards should not be seen by students without parental permission and guidance. If after reviewing the enclosed report card, you would like us to develop a second version of the report card with higher grades, please call XXXXXX at extension XXX.

Does this make your head explode? It does mine. In other words, if after reviewing the report card with your kid's bad grades based upon his true level of achievement, you would like for us to lie to him so his feelings won't be hurt, let us know and we will happily compromise our integrity, the integrity of education itself, and destroy all credibility we have as an educational institution and lie to your child. This is dishonest of the school and it puts the parents in a position of having to explain to the child why the school didn't just tell them the truth to begin with. That is, if the parents bother to actually discuss the bad grades with the children. And how are kids supposed to learn to do better if they never feel the consequences of their own poor performance? This violates so many of the core values I believe we must teach children.

Can you imagine being on the verge of getting fired for your lousy performance on the job, yet you still get a positive performance review? How would you feel if you got fired after receiving a positive performance review because you discovered that they didn't tell you the truth because they were afraid it might hurt your feelings? Surprised? You think? How would you know to improve your performance on the job if you never got an honest review about your work?

Sadly, schools don't feel that children are emotionally equipped to handle bad news, even when that bad news is the truth about their own performance. These kids are not fragile little snowflakes, they are people, and people can handle the truth—they may not like it, but they can handle it, especially if they have been taught to handle it.

Grades are a consequence of performance, and when we rob children of the pain of their consequences, we cheat them of the lesson. In sports, if you can't play the game, you don't make the team. If you are a coach and lose too many games, you get fired. If you are a salesperson who doesn't make any sales, you are a failure at being a sales-person and you lose your job. It is the way life and business works: If you can't do the work, you fail. However, that is not the case in many of our schools. Helicopter parents, bleeding heart school systems, and whiney kids believe they should win whether they can do the work or not.

BEYOND SCHOOL SYSTEMS

Education as a core value means more than just the formal education you receive as the result of attending school. Education is a never-ending process. It's necessary to continue to learn, to be aware, and to stay informed.

You can learn from reading, listening to smart people (you can even learn from stupid people), and, believe it or not, you can learn from watching television. Yes, there is a lot of great stuff on television. The key to what to watch is answering this question: "Does watching this make me smarter or better informed?" If it does, then it just might be something you should pay attention to. Not that you can't just watch television for pure entertainment, too. You just have to pay attention to how much of it you are doing and be aware of what that is keeping you from doing that could have better results.

I recently heard one of the country's leading motiva-tional speakers advise folks to cut themselves off from all news as it can negatively affect your thinking. Just more ridiculous drivel from a so-called thought leader. Maybe that thought leader should have people stop walking on hot coals . . . now there's a thought! Changing a bad situation always begins with awareness of it. If you don't know there is a problem, how can you take the necessary action to solve it? I suggest the opposite: Listen to all sides, then make educated and informed decisions.

Don't bring up bias and start your name calling against various news organizations as a response to this suggestion. If you do, you will have missed the point completely. I listen, watch, and read CNN, Fox, CNBC, MSNBC, ABC, NBC, CBS, NPR, the *New York Times*, *Wall Street Journal*, *Huffington Post*, Yahoo News, Google News, Politico, my local news and newspaper, and more. And then, because I have a brain, I assimilate the information and draw my own conclusions.

And remember folks: You can't be authentically for or against something when all of your information is second or third hand, fed to you by your favorite talking head. Rachel Maddow, Bill O'Reilly, Chris Matthews, Matt Lauer, Megyn Kelly and the rest are interpreters, not reporters. Experience the information for yourself. Are you willing to turn your brain over to someone else? Sadly, far too many are. And you can't claim to be truly informed if all of your information comes from only one biased source.

I find it particularly sad that we are so ill-informed as a society especially because information has never been easier to access. Knowledge is literally at our fingertips, yet we have chosen to invest the bulk of our time in the silly, the useless, and the stupid—things that add nothing to our lives, things that only point us in the wrong direction when we say we want to be successful.

CHAPTER FIVE

WHAT'S WRONG WITH OUR GOVERNMENT

WELCOME TO HELICOPTER AMERICA

I'm sure you've heard the term *helicopter parenting*. Helicopter parents hover around their children in order to protect them from every possible negative thing that could possibly hurt them in any way.

It is also known as overparenting. It is about having too much presence in your child's life. It's about overinvolvement. I know you've witnessed parents who never let their child fail, experience pain, or learn any lesson the hard way.

These parents honestly believe they are helping their children. Deep in their hearts they know their child is better off because they are protecting every aspect of his or her life. If you asked these parents why they are hovering and overparenting and trying to control everything that happens to their child, they would say it is out of love.

Those of us with a little experience and some common sense know that is not the case at all. While these misguided parents might call it love, it's actually child abuse. Yeah, you read it right: child abuse.

Children who are not allowed to experience life as it is, complete with all of the pain and problems, never learn the skills necessary to cope with the pain and problems. Not equipping your children to deal with life as it really is isn't helping them but hurting them.

While this style of parenting has become more prevalent over the last decade or so, it seems that this practice of overinvolvement, overprotection, and I-know-best-what-is-good-for-you has made the leap from being how people parent their children to how government acts toward its citizens.

We have grown from just helicopter parenting to being an entire society plagued by this tragic phenomenon. And this phenomenon has turned our country into what I call Helicopter America.

Weak. Self-absorbed. Hypersensitive. Envious. Afraid. Blaming. Resentful. Anxious. Dependent. Unable to cope. Fragile. Angry.

Those words describe a child who has been raised by helicopter parents. And those words describe society in Helicopter America.

Our government and the people who we elected to run it believe they know better what is good for us than we do. The government is now overly involved and reaching deeper and deeper into our private lives in the name of protecting us when all it is really doing is hurting us.

When asked why, these politicians respond just like the helicopter parent: "It's because we love you, we care about you, and we know what's best for you."

That's laughable to those of us with just a bit of a brain. It's not about love, it's about control. And just like helicopter parenting, it's abuse.

DEAR GOVERNMENT: MIND YOUR OWN BUSINESS!

We need the government out of our bedrooms. Who you sleep with is your business, not the government's.

We need the government out of our kitchens. I will decide what I can eat and whether it's healthy for me or not.

We need the government out of our health care. I will pick my own doctor, and I want to decide who I buy insurance from and even if I want insurance.

We need the government out of our schools. Parents need to be able to choose where their kids go to school, and they need to be able to have input into the curriculum.

We need the government out of our businesses. There should be no business that is too big to fail. I want the government to stop picking winners and losers.

We need the government out of our own houses, too. If I want to smoke in my house that's my business, not the government's.

The government needs to stop taxing my life choices. I am sick of what are commonly known as "sin taxes": sugar taxes, taxes on alcohol and tobacco, taxes on soda, and now the movement to tax meat because it clogs arteries.

At the 2016 Republican Convention, PETA members who were dressed as nuns took to their stilts asking that we tax meat. You honestly can't make this stuff up!

Dear PETA, if you don't want to eat meat, here is an idea: don't. But leave me the hell alone about eating meat. It's my choice, not yours. And the same philosophy applies to smoking, drinking soda, and drinking alcohol. If you don't approve of those things, don't do those things.

That makes perfect sense to me. I don't like baggy pants that ride down around my ass so everyone can see my underwear. The solution for me? Don't wear them.

Everyone please, mind your own damn business. If it doesn't affect you, then leave it alone. Sitting on my patio smoking a cigar with a fine, brown liquor in my hand has no impact on your life. So don't tell me that you don't approve because I don't care what you think.

I promise you that I couldn't care less about what you do in the privacy of your own home. In fact, I don't care about anything you do unless it harms me.

And regardless of either of our lifestyle choices, I sure don't want for either of us to be taxed on them.

WE HAVE TOO MANY LAWS

And we damn sure don't need any new laws until we have first enforced the laws we have.

We don't need any new guns laws. We need to enforce the gun laws we have. We don't need any new immigration laws, either, until we first enforce the immigration laws we already have.

There are laws proposed to make walking and texting illegal. Shouldn't that one be covered by common sense? Do we really need a law?

While I hate texting and driving, I don't believe we need a law that regulates it. Seems to me that the laws we already have for distracted driving should cover cell phone use, including texting.

You can't legislate common sense. You can't legislate intelligence. It is an impossible task and we have to stop trying.

But that's what politicians do. In fact, they are called *lawmakers*. Bad name for them. We have too many law-makers when what we really need are some law-*un*makers.

It is not the role of government to solve all of our problems through legislation. However, we have given it this responsibility because we have so willingly abdicated our own personal responsibility.

It is impossible to legislate good behavior.
Instead, we must both value and teach the core values that create good behavior.

Gun Laws

Full disclosure: I own guns. I have many of them of many types. I have a concealed carry permit. I hunt. I am a member of the National Rifle Association (NRA). I don't agree with much of what the NRA does, but I believe in the right to own firearms and to carry a firearm and want to protect that right.

I know there are some who believe they should be able to strap on their sidearms or carry their AR-15 assault rifles around their necks and walk into a bank or onto an airplane. They believe that the Second Amendment gives them the right to carry whether it makes sense or not. They don't believe there should be any restrictions on gun ownership at any level for anyone. These people are idiots and do not represent responsible gun owners.

And while there are many arguments for more gun control in our country, I firmly believe that guns are not the problem.

It sickens me when a crime of any type happens and the immediate response of many politicians is to blame the gun. Ignore that the guy is a terrorist; the gun made him do it. Ignore the fact that the guy is mentally unstable; it was the gun's fault obviously. Seems that these folks send their brains, logic, and common sense on vacation when they want to assign easy blame, whether it makes sense or not.

After the cop killing in Baton Rouge, Louisiana, in July 2016, Sid Gautreaux, the East Baton Rouge county sheriff said: "To me, this is not so much about gun control as it is about what's in men's hearts. And until we come together as a nation, as a people, to heal as a people . . . if we don't do that and this madness continues we will surely perish."

Once again, education, respect, love, caring, integrity, and the whole list of core values I believe in come into play. If I respect you, I won't commit a crime against you; I won't rob you or break into your house or business. I won't rape you, molest you, assault you, and I won't shoot you. Pretty simple. Where is respect taught? As I have already talked about, it should be taught in our homes, schools, and churches for sure. But also by the way all of us lead our lives every single day.

You might believe my core value approach to gun violence is off course and will take too long and think that the only way to fix things is to pass more laws. We don't need more laws. Laws never completely change behavior. Do speeding laws keep people from speeding? Over 40 million speeding tickets are issued each year. Besides, we have too many laws as it is. And regarding guns, we should start enforcing the gun laws we already have before we start passing more.

You will toss out your statistics about gun violence in the United States and say that because we have more guns, we have more deaths by guns. I could respond in kind with a whole other set of statistics that say registered gun owners commit a very small percentage of crimes and that statistically when gun ownership rises, gun violence decreases. I could use Australia and England and other countries to make my point about what happens when you take guns away from the citizens. Here's the problem: we can all make statistics prove any point we want to. We watch it happen every day on the news and hear it from our politicians. So let's move past the statistics and arguments and just rely on a little common sense.

After the police shooting in Louisiana, I posted something about how I hate that people think that shooting cops is a solution. I hate that cops have become targets. I hate that guns will be blamed. And I said much more about the situation. I got a lot of support for my words but also got a lot of vitriol in return as well. Some of the responses were from the anti-gun rights people. I respect their right to disagree. I will defend their right to their opinion and their First Amendment right to express that opinion. I wish they were as supportive of my Second Amendment rights as I am of their First Amendment rights. One poster on my page had one of the best responses I have read to a person who suggested that we completely outlaw all guns.

Karen Farris Sellick responded to this person who wanted to completely outlaw all guns with this: "You are right on point. But not only should we ban guns, but also large trucks that can drive over hundreds of people, airplanes that can be flown into buildings and kill thousands of people, anything that could possibly be used to make a bomb that can be strapped to one's person and blow up hundreds of people like those evil fertilizer factories, those websites and manuals that teach people how to easily build bombs for mass destruction, chemicals that can poison people, matches that can be used to light a fuse, knives that can stab, etc. All of these organizations and manufacturers have blood on their hands and should be ashamed of themselves! After all, it is the object, not the person, that kills. Murderers have no other options than guns, and without access to guns, there would be no more murders, people would simply change their evil ways and give up, except, of course, for all of those events in France and other countries where guns are outlawed, where that murderous truck was used and all of those pesky suicide bombers have blown people up over and over again. But let's focus on getting rid of the guns first, then we will tackle all of the others weapons later. First things first."

Blaming guns for violence is like blaming forks for obesity. It's like blaming a pencil for misspelled words. A gun is just a tool. Nothing more. A gun can be used for good or for bad—it's the person who makes the choice. Besides, it's always interesting to me when politicians want to outlaw guns but are protected by people carrying guns. Rep. Charlie Rangel, that paragon of honesty, integrity, and ethics, recently said that law-abiding citizens shouldn't have to carry a gun for protection but that politicians deserve and need to be protected by guns. Once again, political hypocrisy reigns supreme.

I hate worn-out, bumper sticker clichés but sometimes they make sense: "When you outlaw guns, only outlaws will have guns." True. For you folks who want all guns outlawed, wake up. You aren't getting guns out of the hands of bad guys. Ever. Did outlawing liquor during Prohibition get liquor off the streets? No, it just turned liquor production over to the bad guys. Bad guys are always going to have guns. How about giving the good guys a fighting chance?

Because I don't blame guns but blame people, I do think we need better background checks to make sure that the wrong people do not get access to guns. And we need more personal responsibility by others to keep guns out of the hands of unstable family members. Again, that's just common sense.

Speaking of common sense, there is a movement to hold gun manufacturers liable for gun violence. Oh yeah, that makes perfect sense to me. Are we going to hold Jack Daniels and Coors liable for crimes related to drunkenness? General Motors liable for car accidents? McDonald's liable for diabetes? Please. This makes no sense. Don't get caught up in the emotion of the moment like antigun politicians want you to do. Personal responsibility needs to come into play. Not everything is someone else's fault and blaming them is not the answer.

So folks, use your heads and consider these points:

- When a responsible, licensed gun owner carries a gun into a public place, you are safer for it.

- Gun-free zones are targets. If you know no one there has any ability to fight back, those people are weak in the eyes of a bad guy.
- Guns are a tool. You don't blame a hammer or outlaw hammers when someone is killed with a hammer. It's the user that kills and anything can become a weapon in the hands of the wrong person.
- Outlawing guns will not make us safer. In fact, it will only make our society more dangerous.
- Before believing any politician or Facebook meme or talking head on television (or even me) about gun statistics, do some research. Then fact-check that research. Then use your head.
- If you choose to carry a gun, get a permit, get training, practice, and be careful. It is a tremendous responsibility that should not be taken lightly.
- Some people are just f-ing crazy! There is no other explanation. In many cases, there is no "why" other than that they are insane and want to kill people. If they didn't have a gun, they would use a baseball bat or an ax or a car.

POLITICS AND POLITICIANS

We need to get political action committees and big money out of our elections. Let the people support the party and the candidate of their choosing. Our elections are up for sale and typically the one with the most money wins.

As for politicians, I am tired of people who complain about politicians, failing to realize "they are us." Politicians reflect us. They reflect our core values. We vote in crooks because we are crooked. We vote in thieves, liars, and cheats because that's what we have become.

Our government at every level is a reflection of us.

The government spends more money than it takes in. Forty-three percent of Americans spend more money than they earn, too.

The government has no surplus, in real people terms; that means no savings. Most Americans don't have any savings, either.

The government has too much debt and so does the average American.

Politicians and the government are a direct reflection of who we are as individuals.

Before you attack "them" go look in the mirror and realize that "them" is us.

Partisanship

We have gotten to the point where we feel that the other side never has a good idea. How can that be? Do Republicans really believe that Democrats are always wrong about everything? Do Democrats really believe that about Republicans? I don't think so. I just can't think so. Surely one side sees some value in some of the positions of the other side. Yet we have become so divided that the divisiveness has caused us all to become blind and deaf to the reasonable words of the other side simply because they come from the other side. Even if one side did agree with the other, it would be afraid to admit it because its voting base wouldn't approve.

When some conservatives use words like "libtard" to describe people with a liberal point of view and when liberals communicate that conservatives are racist and homophobic, we have lost our way. And please don't doubt that we have indeed lost our way. This name-calling and the stereotypes are not helping us create a better country or better citizens. This relates to what I spoke about earlier around the topic of meanness. It revolves around the core value of respect. We must grow beyond all of this hyperpartisanship.

I view myself as a pretty typical American. I have some extremely conservative views and I have some extremely liberal views. I am extremely conservative when it comes to money. I believe that you can have whatever you want as long as you can afford to pay for it without going into debt. When you are debt free, have a surplus in the bank, and your bills are all paid, then buy it. That rule should apply to government as well as individuals and families. Sadly, that is viewed as a conservative position politically. I also believe that you can marry whomever you want and the government should stay out of it. That is considered a liberal point of view. Both of those positions will lose me followers, readers, and fans. I don't care. At all. All of this is to say that I fall pretty much in the middle politically. Which means I don't have anybody to vote for that I can fully support. The liberal candidates are too liberal for me and the conservative candidates are too conservative. Moderate is a position, and those of us who are, are left wanting.

Instead, we have a partisan government that swings every few years too far right and then too far left. We need to come together on more issues. We need to value both sides of an argument. We need to listen and show respect for each other and stop being so damn mean about everything.

By the way, folks, not everything is political. If I get a traffic ticket, it's not Obama's fault. If I go on Facebook and post how hot it is, I don't need some nimrod bringing up George W. Bush. Not everything can be blamed on Bush, Clinton(s), Obama, Trump, or any other political figure. So stop ascribing your stupid partisan politics to everything that is going on in the world. You aren't helping things. In fact, you are making things worse!

We are a divided nation. Young from old. Blacks from whites. Left from right. Republicans from Democrats. Elitists from the common man. It has to stop. If it doesn't, we are doomed.

Voting and Voters

I post things on social media about the importance of voting and there is always some asshat that chimes in with how voting doesn't matter. If you believe that, you are too stupid to fog a mirror. Voting matters. And if you choose not to participate in the process, you are too stupid to have an opinion and I have nothing to say to you about anything going on in our country.

And the old lesser of two evils argument is equally idiotic. Just go ahead and vote for the lesser of two evils. If you don't, people even dumber than you just might elect the one who is more evil. Apathy is never a solution.

And how do you know who to vote for? How about doing a little research? It's not that hard, you know. And please don't think that watching Fox or MSNBC is doing research. Talking heads on partisan, opinion-based television is not research. Neither is watching the late night talks shows. Or reading the tabloids while in line at the supermarket.

Check out the candidates' voting records if they have them. Past behavior is still the best predictor of future behavior. So look at what they have said and done and then figure out what they will likely do based on that. Read their position and policy statements on their websites. Then determine which candidate you should vote for based on all of this information. Notice I used the word information. Try casting a vote based on actual information and watch what a difference you will see happen over time in our government.

Don't be an uninformed idiot who casts his vote based only on what the candidate is saying or your favorite talking head says. Please be smarter than that.

And don't vote for someone simply because the candidate is the right color or gender. Bet I stepped on some toes with that line, didn't I? If you put color or gender above honesty, integrity, competence, and policy, you are too stupid to be trusted with the sacred honor of being able to cast a vote. Shame on you.

Politicians are simply a reflection of the people who elect them. They are no better and no worse than the people who cast their votes for them. We can't expect to have better politicians until we become better people.

If I Were President

I get a lot of people who post on my social media, "Larry Winget for President!" I appreciate the thoughts behind the sentiment but I can assure you that I would never do it. I have no interest in becoming president of the United States. I will readily admit that I am too selfish. I wish more good people would do it, but I am not going to be one of them. However, if I could be king, I would gladly take on that role! And here is what I would do:

- A 10 percent, across-the-board cut on *all* government spending. Everyone and everything in government bites the bullet equally, with no playing favorites. There is plenty of waste in government and 10 percent is a great starting place.
- Incentivize businesses to grow, hire, create, and manufacture. You can fix a whole lot that is wrong with our country by putting more people back to work. Cut taxes, realign health care, and get off the backs of small business.
- Create a path to citizenship for undocumented immigrants already here who wish to do the work, be here legally, and pay taxes. And all companies pay taxes on *all* employees. No under the table BS anymore.
- Stop paying members of Congress forever and cut lifetime benefits. Plus, they live by the same laws we do. And they must vote on everything put before them without exception. Their only job is to vote, so vote or get fired. All votes will be posted online for everyone to see. Complete transparency.
- Two terms maximum for everyone and then you go back to work. No more lifetime politicians.
- Entitlements must be reigned in. We cannot sustain the increasing dependency on government. Period.

CHAPTER SIX

THE BIG QUESTION: ARE WE ABLE TO TURN ALL THIS AROUND?

Of course we are. We are able to turn it all around at every level. None of what I have described has to be the way it is. We don't have to be in the mess I have described here. Take hope in this statement. It doesn't have to be this way.

I have no doubt that we are strong enough to make the changes it will take to fix it all. Why? Because none of what it will take is all that hard. That's actually the issue. As my mentor Jim Rohn said, "What is easy to do is just as easy not to do."

That is the problem moving forward. It would actually be fairly easy to do what it takes to fix these things. Which means the question is not, "Are we *able* to turn this all around." The question is, "Are we *willing* to turn this all around?"

Are you willing to do whatever it takes in order to get what you want? You are able to do all of it, but are you willing?

The only thing standing between you and what you want is you and what you aren't willing to do.

IN YOUR BUSINESS

As a manager and leader, are you willing to fire people who don't do what they are paid to do? Are you willing to take a stand for what's right even though taking a stand will be unpopular?

Are you willing to show up on time? Are you willing to work the whole time you are on the job like you promised you would do when you were hired? Are you willing to serve your customers even when your customer isn't being pleasant or fair? Are you willing to be honest in every transaction with your employees and customers?

IN YOUR FAMILY

Are you willing to take the time to teach your children about money? About how to earn it, save it, invest it, and be charitable with it?

Are you willing to teach them about treating people fairly?

Are you willing to have the tough conversations about sex and race and respect?

Are you willing to show them through your own actions all of the traits and values you want them to have as adults?

Are you willing to listen to your kids and your spouse?

Are you willing to teach your children how to not only survive but thrive in the real world by teaching them real world skills?

Are you willing to kick your adult children out of your house and honor them and love them enough to expect them to be self-reliant?

Are you willing to stop being an enabler to them?

IN YOUR OWN LIFE

Are you willing to walk away from those people you call friends who are only moving you further away from where you say you want to be? Are you ready to kick all toxic people out of your life?

Are you willing to be honest with yourself about how hard you work?

Are you willing to turn off the television and read a book that might actually help you be a better person, better in business, a better parent or spouse, or better with your money?

Are you willing to stop spending money on things you don't need?

Are you willing to save your money so you won't have to rely on anyone when retirement comes around?

Are you willing to be nice and kind and generous with your time, money, and judgment?

ARE YOU WILLING TO LIVE BY THESE CORE VALUES?

Honesty
Integrity
Respect

Work ethic
Adding value
Fiscal responsibility
Education
Kindness
Self-sufficiency

If you are willing not only to say it but to do it, then we can turn things around.

YOU CAN'T CHANGE THE WORLD

I know that is contradictory to what the motivational bozos say, but once again, those poor things are totally wrong and living in la-la land. The world will change when it wants to, not when you want it to. Right now it doesn't want to. Maybe it never will. You can't change the government except with your vote. You can't change the price of gasoline. You can't change the way your friends are, either. Like the world, the other people in your life will change when they want to, not when you want them to. In reality, you can't change much of anything. However . . .

Here's what you *can* do: change *your* world. You can do the things I suggested at the end of each chapter to get back to your own core values. You can teach core values to your kids. You can focus every day on letting these core values drive your action, your words, and your thoughts. You can run your business according to your core values. You can handle your money according to your core values. You can vote your core values. You can parent according to your core values. You can live your core values in all that you say and do. Do that, and *your* world will change. And if enough of us do it, then maybe, slowly, with enough time, the world actually will change.

There is a Cherokee legend, known as the Parable of the Two Wolves. It says there is a fight that goes on inside of every person—a fight between two wolves. One wolf is evil and angry. It is full of resentment, pride, arrogance, lies, meanness, and ego. The other wolf is full of love, peace, joy, humility, kindness, generosity, truth, and compassion. Which wolf wins the fight? The wolf you feed.

These two wolves are fighting right now at every level of our society. Which one will win? The one we feed.

ABOUT THE AUTHOR

Larry Winget is a best-selling author, television personality, social commentator, and internationally acclaimed speaker.

He has written six *New York Times* and *Wall Street Journal* best-selling books that have been translated into over 20 languages, including *Shut Up, Stop Whining and Get a Life*; *You're Broke Because You Want to Be*; *It's Called Work for a Reason*; *People Are Idiots and I Can Prove It*; *Your Kids Are Your Own Fault*; and *Grow a Pair: How to Stop Being a Victim and Take Back Your Life, Your Business, and Your Sanity*.

Larry has starred in his own television series on A&E, two PBS specials, and two CNBC specials. He has appeared on *Dr. Phil*, the *Today* show, *Tool Academy*, *The Big Idea*, *Larry King Live*, and in three national television commercials. Larry appears regularly on many national television news shows speaking on the topics of success, business, personal finance, parenting, and the wussification of America. Larry is also a member of the Speaker Hall of Fame. Find out more at www.larrywinget.com.